Creative Theme Parties

Dining Adventures
for Friends to Share

by Shari Shields

Technigraphic Systems, Inc.
Edmonds, Washington

Technigraphic Systems Inc.
111 James Street
Edmonds, WA 98020
(206) 672-2963 • FAX (206) 775-5727
Printed and bound in the United States of America
First Edition
First Printing, September 1993
ISBN: 0-9633591-1-8
Library of Congress Catalog Card Number: 93-61214

◆ ACKNOWLEDGMENTS ◆

This book is a product of the many good times and special memories our own Gourmet Grub Club has created together. My thanks to Paula and Nick Prebezac, Kelli and Dan Ambrosi, Martine and Chris Fabrizio, and my husband, Jonathan, with extra thanks to Nick, Kelli, and Martine for their boundless creativity and commitment.

In the beginning, I envisioned The Gourmet Grub Club as a way to bring friends together in pursuit of the pleasures of cooking and entertaining—to learn together, to grow together, and to have a great time. In our case, all this has come to pass, plus much more, thanks to the talent, dedication, and friendship of this very special group of people.

◆ TABLE OF CONTENTS ◆

◆ INTRODUCTION ◆

*F*ood and friendship are two of life's greatest pleasures, which is why we love parties—that quintes-
sential pairing of these two elements. Planning, preparing,
and ultimately sharing a truly memorable party can be a
tremendous source of satisfaction. As we all know, it can
also involve a fair amount of time, work, and expense,
especially if we're trying to handle it all ourselves.

In our busy world, too often it's the things that bring us
the most pleasure that get postponed, or worse yet, elimi-
nated. But memorable parties are possible, with planning
and participation. The theme parties in this book provide
the plan, and your friends supply the participation. Everyone has a good time.

Originally this book was intended as a sequel to our first
book, The Gourmet Grub Club—A Guide to Cooking and
Entertaining With Your Friends, which outlines a plan for
forming your own gourmet dining club. Of course, we hope
that readers of the first book and all the other dining clubs
in existence find material and inspiration in these pages.
But our parties stand alone as well, and can work for you
any time you feel like doing something special for yourself
and your friends.

WHAT IS A GRUB CLUB PARTY?

Each of the twelve theme parties we've chosen to feature in this book is a unique dining adventure. Several of the themes are based on international cuisine and customs. Parties such as the **Greek Feast** and the **East Indian Escapade** explore the fascinating food and culture of these countries. Other themes are inspired by the seasons, such as the **Spring Fling** and the **New England Autumn**, while **A Christmas Carol** is our toast to the holidays.

We even travel back in time, to the **Nifty Fifties**. Our parties run the gamut from the supercasual **Superbowl Sunday**, to the ultra-chic **Elegant Interlude.** There's something for everybody, and we hope that you try each and every one.

BEYOND THE POTLUCK

Guests bringing dishes to a dinner party is hardly a new idea, but we've taken the traditional potluck concept a few steps further. The standard potluck arrangement involves random contributions—one person brings a salad, another brings a dessert, and so on. Granted, everyone gets fed, but there's no guarantee that you'll end up with a pleasantly coordinated meal.

Alternatively, Grub Club menus are designed to work as a whole. Our menus are divided into a series of four courses, which we call "acts." If you imagine your party as a theatrical production, with a provocative opening, a gradual building of action, a climax, and a satisfying conclusion, then you understand the logic of presenting foods in a manner that tells a story. There are many similarities between entertaining at home and entertaining in the theatrical sense.

In our menus, **Act I** is the Hors D'Oeuvre and Cocktail course. Its purpose is to stimulate appetites and get everyone into the spirit of the event. This course is usually served away from the dining room table. It includes one or two hors d'oeuvres, plus a cocktail, punch, wine, or other beverage that is relevant to the theme.

Act II proceeds to the dining room. This is the Appetizer course, and includes some type of soup, salad, or other appetizer, plus bread and a corresponding wine or beverage.

Act III is the Main Course, and includes a main dish and corresponding side dishes, plus a wine selection carefully chosen to complement the main dish. This is the heart of the meal, or the climax.

Act IV is the Dessert course—the satisfying conclusion. The dessert is accompanied by coffee, and an after-dinner drink, which we refer to as the "curtain call."

As you plan your party, each "act" is assigned to a participant, a participating couple, or a "team." These people are responsible for the preparation and serving of all recipes and beverages involved in their "act." You, as the host, are responsible for Act III—the Main Course—as well as for orchestrating all the "extras" that complete the party experience.

You and your guests are cast, crew, and audience of your own production. As a joint venture, you all deserve applause for its success. Entertaining has never been so much fun!

THE BIG PICTURE

A Grub Club party is a total sensory experience. You will notice that each of the themes in this book includes entertaining ideas that help to set the scene. Decor, lighting, and your table setting combine to create a special ambience that sets your party apart from all others. The right music can be an effective mood enhancer. Costumes or special attire can promote "esprit de corps," and look great in photographs. We also suggest activities that can be incorporated into your parties, from wine-tastings, to games, to gift exchanges. A great party is the sum of its parts, and most of these suggestions can be executed with a minimum of time or expense.

ABOUT OUR RECIPES

Each recipe in this book is designed to feed eight people, and each menu provides a substantial meal for a party of that size. If you have fewer than eight guests, you may double up on "acts," eliminate a recipe or two, or cut recipes as you see fit. If your party includes more than eight guests, you may divide the "acts" up, add a dish or two of your own choosing, or increase the quantities of certain recipes.

Our recipes are created for maximum enjoyment. We believe in the best quality ingredients—fresh herbs and produce whenever possible, plus the best quality olive oils, real butter, real maple syrup, and the like. We believe that an occasional exercise in indulgence is good for the soul, and that the reward for time spent cooking should be pure and unadulterated pleasure.

In the case of our ethnic and international menus, we've presented recipes that are authentic in feeling and flavor, yet are accessible to American kitchens. You may have to search a little for some of the ingredients, but that is part of the fun. Many supermarkets have begun stocking a wide range of ethnic ingredients, and most cities have a variety of ethnic specialty stores. Also, many of these ingredients are available by mail order. Check our Mail Order Source Guide on page 165 of this book for options.

We hope that many of these recipes will become staples in your cooking repertoire, as they have in ours.

ABOUT GOURMET DINING CLUBS

If you are already a member of a gourmet dining club, then you've already discovered how much fun it is is to gather on a regular basis to share good food and good times with good friends. If you are not yet a member of a club, but enjoy cooking and entertaining, then perhaps you should consider starting a club of your own.

You don't have to be an accomplished cook to enjoy the benefits of belonging to a gourmet dining club. Indeed, one of the main reasons for joining a club of this type is to learn more about cooking, and to try out new recipes and techniques with a "support group" to cheer you along. This was our incentive for forming our original Gourmet Grub Club. We have all learned a great deal together, and look forward to new challenges as we continue to explore our capabilities.

Another wonderful benefit of belonging to a gourmet dining club is the spirit of camaraderie and the sense of family that develops over time. I've talked to groups that have been together for decades. Such histories they boast, and what wonderful stories they have to share! Throughout all of life's ups and downs, these clubs have provided continuity and comfort to their members—a place to belong.

If you are interested in forming your own club, our book, *The Gourmet Grub Club—A Guide to Cooking and Entertaining With Your Friends* will tell you all you need to know to set the wheels in motion and keep things running. Check the back of this book for ordering information.

In the meantime, have fun with the parties in this book, and remember, entertaining is a piece of cake when everyone puts on an apron!

◆ ◆ ◆
Superbowl Sunday

Act I

Kickoff Crunch

Touchdown Chicken Wings

Spiked Gator Bowl

◆

Act II

Scrimmage Salad

Beer

◆

Act III

Halftime Heroes

Beer

◆

Act IV

Superbowl Sundaes

Brandy or Tawny Port

◆ SUPERBOWL SUNDAY ◆

*A*ttention, sports fans! This is the event you've been
waiting for! The biggest game of the season plus
plenty of great gridiron grub is every armchair quarterback's
dream come true.

No Superbowl gathering would be complete without an
ample supply of edibles to keep the TV troops cheering. Our
lineup features make-ahead munchies that get you out of
the kitchen in no time, and back in front of the television
where you belong. Get ready to pass the Kickoff Crunch,
tackle some hearty Halftime Heroes, and celebrate (or con-
sole) with outrageous Superbowl Sundaes. And don't forget
lots of ice cold beer or some refreshing Spiked Gator Bowl
punch to wash it all down.

Our game plan is a sure winner for a super good time, on
Superbowl Sunday or whenever you have a team of hungry
friends to feed.

DECOR

No candles or flowers or fancy place settings for this crowd. A casual, practical approach is the goal here. Decorate simply in the colors of the team you're rooting for (or both teams' colors, if loyalties are divided). Crepe paper streamers and balloons are bright and bold embellishments. In addition, many stores offer Superbowl memorabilia and party gear, such as plastic football-shaped trays for chips, mini-pompoms, and posters.

Most of the eating activity will take place in front of the television, so you will need to set up a buffet table for serving. A bright green tablecloth with "goal lines" made from white crepe paper streamers creates a perfect arena for your Superbowl fare. Offer sturdy paper plates, plastic cups, and generous paper napkins for no-fumble munching and easy post-game cleanup.

ATTIRE

Dress for casual comfort in your team's colors. Jeans, sweatshirts, and jerseys are perfect for lounging in front of the tube, or a rough-and-tumble game of touch football on the lawn.

Female fans might consider donning their old cheerleader or pep squad uniforms.

MUSIC

Between the pre-game show, the game itself, and post-game highlights, count on the television being tuned in for most of the day. You can give your stereo a rest for this event.

ACTIVITIES

No Superbowl would be complete without some betting (millions of dollars are wagered each year) so be sure and set up a football pool. Stores actually sell special kits for this important activity. Also, award a prize to the fan who comes closest to guessing the winning score.

◆ ACT I ◆

KICKOFF CRUNCH

*Americans consume literally tons of popcorn on Superbowl Sunday.
We combine our share with special seasonings and crunchy goodies.*

2 quarts freshly popped unsalted popcorn

1 1¾-ounce can shoestring potatoes

1 1¾-ounce can fried onions

1 cup pretzel sticks

1 cup honey-roasted mixed nuts

⅓ cup butter, melted

1 tsp. Worcestershire sauce

½ tsp. lemon pepper

¼ tsp. garlic powder

¼ tsp. onion powder

◆ Preheat oven to 325°.

◆ Combine popcorn, shoestring potatoes, fried onions, pretzels, and mixed nuts in a roasting pan. Set aside.

◆ Combine melted butter with seasonings in a small bowl. Pour over popcorn mixture and stir until evenly coated.

◆ Bake 8 to 10 minutes, stirring once or twice. Cool completely. Store in an airtight container.

SPIKED GATOR BOWL

Our version of the ever-popular gridiron thirst-quencher, with a kick!

1 12-ounce can frozen lemonade

1 12-ounce can frozen limeade

1 2-liter bottle 7-Up

½ cup sugar (to taste)

2 lemons, thinly sliced

2 limes, thinly sliced

1 fifth vodka, chilled

yellow and green food coloring

◆ In a punch bowl, mix lemonade and limeade concentrates with water (using amounts recommended on can directions).

◆ Stir in sugar, 7-Up, and vodka. Add a few drops each of yellow and green food coloring—just enough to give your punch a "glow."

◆ Float lemon and lime slices on top.

 Grub Club Tip
Minus the vodka, this makes a refreshing punch for non-drinkers.

TOUCHDOWN CHICKEN WINGS

A party treat that's sure to score!

4 pounds chicken wings, separated at joints
2 cups milk
1 tsp. bottled hot pepper sauce
½ tsp. cayenne pepper
1 tsp. seasoned salt
1 tsp. lemon pepper
Zesty Hot Sauce (recipe follows)
Cool Blue Cheese Dip (recipe follows)

◆ Wash chicken thoroughly and pat dry.

◆ In a medium bowl, combine milk, hot pepper sauce, and cayenne pepper. Add chicken and stir to coat. Cover and refrigerate overnight.

◆ The next day, drain chicken. Rinse and pat dry. Arrange in a shallow baking pan and sprinkle with seasoned salt and lemon pepper.

◆ Bake at 400° for 30 minutes. Transfer wings to a bowl and cover with Zesty Hot Sauce (recipe follows). (If making ahead, cool, cover, and refrigerate until serving time.)

◆ Before serving, preheat broiler to 450°. Arrange wings on a broiling pan. Broil for 7 minutes. Turn and baste with remaining Hot Sauce. Broil for 7 minutes more.

◆ Serve with Cool Blue Cheese Dip (recipe follows) and lots of napkins!

Zesty Hot Sauce
½ cup cider vinegar
¾ cup beer
¼ cup tomato sauce
¼ cup tomato paste
1 tsp. bottled hot pepper sauce
2 cloves garlic, pressed
3 Tbsp. sugar
1 jalapeño pepper, minced
Salt and pepper to taste

◆ Combine all ingredients in a medium saucepan. Bring to a boil over medium heat. Reduce heat and simmer for 45 minutes, stirring occasionally.

Cool Blue Cheese Dip
4 ounces blue cheese, crumbled
1 cup sour cream
½ cup mayonnaise
½ tsp. dry mustard

◆ Combine all ingredients. Cover and refrigerate until serving.

◆ ACT II ◆

SCRIMMAGE SALAD

Salad ingredients are arranged in neat rows on a field of chopped lettuce, then drizzled with a tangy vinaigrette dressing.

1 large head romaine or Boston lettuce, chopped into small pieces

2 medium sweet red peppers, diced

1 cup frozen baby peas, thawed

1 6-ounce can pitted ripe olives, cut into quarters

1 cup diced jicama

2 medium carrots, diced

1 cup diced fresh mushrooms

1 6-ounce can black beans, rinsed and drained

Tangy Vinaigrette

½ cup balsamic vinegar

¼ cup olive oil

¼ cup vegetable oil

1 shallot, finely minced

½ tsp. dry mustard

¼ tsp. salt (or to taste)

fresh ground pepper to taste

◆ To make dressing, put all ingredients in a jar with a tight-fitting lid. Shake well to mix. Refrigerate several hours or overnight.

◆ To make salad, prepare vegetables, keeping each in a separate bowl.

◆ On a large serving platter or medium rectangular tray, make a bed of chopped lettuce. Arrange vegetables on top in uniform rows in the order given above. (Start with the middle row and work outward, for best results).

◆ Cover with plastic wrap and refrigerate until serving. Just before serving, remove plastic wrap and drizzle with Tangy Vinaigrette. Do not toss.

Grub Club Tip

You may substitute other salad ingredients for the ones given, making sure you have one cup of each ingredient. Aim for lots of contrast in color and flavor. Some alternatives are kidney or garbanzo beans; corn; green or yellow peppers; diced celery, apple, or cucumber; or quartered cherry tomatoes.

Beverage

Beer is the popular choice among the Superbowl set. You may want to have a bottle or two of white or rosé jug wine on hand to please any non-beer drinkers, and perhaps some nonalcoholic beer, sodas, and seltzers as well.

◆ ACT III ◆

HALFTIME HEROES

Hearty, substantial sandwiches to satisfy even the most manly appetite.

8 French rolls

2 green peppers, sliced crosswise into ⅛-inch slices

2 medium onions, sliced

2 Tbsp. vegetable oil

1 pound Monterey Jack cheese, sliced

8 pitted ripe olives

Sauce

1 29-ounce can tomato sauce

1 6-ounce can tomato paste

¼ cup brown sugar

1 Tbsp. vinegar

2 cloves garlic, pressed

¼ cup chopped fresh parsley

2 tsp. oregano

¼ tsp. cayenne pepper

Meatballs

1 pound lean ground beef

½ pound hot Italian sausage

1 cup soft bread crumbs

1 egg

¼ cup milk

½ medium onion, minced

4 cloves garlic, pressed

1 tsp. Worcestershire sauce

1½ tsp. dry mustard

½ tsp. thyme

1 tsp. salt

½ tsp. pepper

◆ The day before the event, make the meatballs. In a medium bowl, beat the egg and milk. Stir in the minced onion, garlic, Worcestershire sauce, dry mustard, thyme, salt and pepper. Add bread crumbs, ground beef, and sausage. Mix well.

◆ Roll meat mixture into 2-inch diameter logs. Cut into 2-inch slices and round into balls. Place in a 13 x 9-inch baking dish or pan.

◆ Bake in a 375° oven for 25 to 30 minutes. Drain off fat. Cool, cover, and refrigerate.

◆ On the day of the event, make the sauce. Combine all sauce ingredients in a large saucepan. Simmer for 30 minutes. Add meatballs and heat through.

◆ Preheat the oven broiler to 450°.

◆ Sauté the sliced onions and green peppers in oil over medium heat until soft.

◆ Slice the French rolls in half lengthwise. Scoop about ½-inch of bread from the bottom halves with your fingers. Toast bread halves under oven broiler for a minute or so until lightly browned. Remove.

◆ Place 3 or 4 meatballs on each bottom half, topping with extra sauce. Cover with sautéed onions and green peppers, and slices of cheese.

◆ Broil until cheese is melted and bubbly. Cover with tops of rolls and secure with olive-speared toothpicks.

 Grub Club Tip
Light eaters may prefer their sandwiches open-face, using only half a roll.

Beverage
Continue with beer, jug wines, etc. for this course.

◆ ACT IV ◆

SUPERBOWL SUNDAES

A post-game highlight.

½ gallon vanilla ice cream   Raspberry Sauce (recipe follows)
Super Brownies (recipe follows)

◆ Place a brownie in the bottom of individual dessert dishes. Top with a couple of scoops of ice cream, and drizzle with Raspberry Sauce.

Super Brownies

5 squares (1-ounce each) unsweetened chocolate, cut into pieces
⅔ cup butter
1¾ cup sugar

2 tsp. vanilla
3 eggs
1 cup flour
¾ cup chopped nuts
½ cup semi-sweet chocolate chips

◆ Preheat oven to 350°.

◆ Heat unsweetened chocolate and butter in the top of a double boiler over medium heat, stirring constantly until melted and smooth. Remove from heat and cool slightly.

◆ In a large bowl, beat sugar, vanilla, and eggs with an electric mixer on high for 5 minutes. Beat in melted chocolate on low speed, and then flour, until blended. Fold in nuts and chocolate chips.

◆ Spread into a greased 9 x 9 x 2-inch baking pan. Bake for 40 to 45 minutes until brownies pull away from the sides of the pan. Cool completely before cutting into squares.

Raspberry Sauce

2 12-ounce packages frozen
raspberries, thawed

⅔ cup sugar

⅔ cup currant jelly

2 Tbsp. lemon juice

◆ Purée the raspberries in a blender or food processor. Pour the purée into a wire mesh strainer set over a bowl and press through with a rubber spatula to remove seeds. Discard seeds.

◆ In a medium saucepan, combine the purée with the sugar, currant jelly, and lemon juice. Cook and stir over medium heat until thoroughly blended. Raise the heat to high and boil, stirring constantly, for 2 minutes.

◆ Remove from heat. Skim any foam from surface. Pour into a jar or other container and cool. Cover and refrigerate until serving.

Coffee
Coffee for this event should be robust—no prissy flavored varieties and nothing decaffeinated. Serve in hefty mugs.

Curtain Call
Wind down your Superbowl festivities with a glass of brandy, or tawny port.

NOTES

_____

_____

_____

_____

_____

_____

_____

_____

_____

_____

Elegant Interlude

Act I

Rumaki

Baked Camembert with Ruby Relish

Champagne

◆

Act II

Tossed Salad Elegante

French Bread Croutons

Orvietto Classico or Vernaccia

◆

Act III

Baked Chicken with Poached Oranges

Julienned Carrots with Thyme

Pinot Noir or Beaujolais-Villages

◆

Act IV

Chocolate Mint Mousse

Cognac or Brandy

◆ Elegant Interlude ◆

*T*his is the theme to choose when you're in the mood for something truly special. It's a "grown-up" dinner party with all the accoutrements—an opportunity to expose the romantic side of your personality and to indulge your most glamorous fantasies.

Candlelight, roses, and sparkling champagne are just a few of the sensual delights that await you. Proudly display your good china and crystal, or whatever else you most cherish. This is a time to revel in all that is luxurious. After all, nothing is too good for you and your friends.

"Elegant Interlude" is a perfect way to celebrate Valentine's Day, or a friend's engagement, or any occasion that calls for something extravagant and exquisite. But then, why wait for an excuse?

DECOR

Let your imagination soar and your event will be an evening to remember. Romance your dining room table with a lovely lace tablecloth and fold your napkins with artistic flair. Lay a rose across each dinner plate. (Silk roses are often a less expensive alternative to fresh roses, and may be "recycled"). Place vases of roses in the center of the table, or anywhere else they might be enjoyed. A single bloom in a bud vase is a classic expression of good taste, and easy on the budget. Candles are all-important in creating romantic ambience; tall tapers are especially dramatic. If possible, candlelight should be your only source of illumination.

Float paper-thin lemon slices in glasses of ice water and be lavish with garnishes on all your dishes. Hand-lettered place cards are a tasteful touch, as are individual menus, rolled into scrolls and tied with ribbons. Accessory pieces that you own or have access to, perhaps a silver champagne bucket or crystal decanter, are the "pièces de résistance."

ATTIRE

In keeping with the spirit of glamour and elegance, dress accordingly in suits and ties, dresses and heels, and jewelry that sparkles in candlelight. Dressing luxuriously can be a great mood enhancer, and is a fitting tribute to a festive occasion. If your group is celebrating Valentine's Day, everyone must wear something red.

MUSIC

Classical piano, a string quartet, or gentle harp music will provide lyrical accompaniment to your magical evening. The library offers a wealth of suitable selections in the classical music category.

ACTIVITIES

Dining and dancing go together like moonlight and romance. Have your group take a beginning ballroom dancing class, or engage an instructor for the evening (perhaps a friend or a club member?) to lead the group in some basic steps. Dancing (like cooking) is a wonderful activity for couples to share.

◆ ACT I ◆

RUMAKI

Rumaki are traditionally made with chicken livers. This updated version simply uses chicken.

6 boneless, skinless chicken thighs, cut into ¾ inch pieces

16 slices bacon, cut in half

8 green onions, cut into 2-inch pieces

32 canned whole water chestnuts (one 5-ounce can)

Marinade

½ cup soy sauce

½ tsp. ground ginger

1 tsp. curry powder

2 cloves garlic, minced

¼ cup dry sherry

◆ Combine marinade ingredients. Marinate chicken for 1 to 2 hours.

◆ Wrap a shrimp, a piece of green onion, and a water chestnut in a half piece of bacon. Secure with a wooden toothpick. Continue until all ingredients are used. Place Rumaki in a shallow baking dish and pour marinade over. Cover and marinate at least one hour.

◆ Before serving, preheat broiler to 500°. Transfer Rumaki to a broiling pan. Broil for 5 to 10 minutes, turning at least once, until bacon is thoroughly cooked. Transfer to a serving platter and serve hot.

BAKED CAMEMBERT WITH RUBY RELISH

A sweet-and-sour red pepper relish tops warm, creamy Camembert. This recipe was developed by our friend, Diana McLeod, who cans great quantities of the Ruby Relish to have on hand. This recipe is one of our favorites.

2 cups coarsely chopped sweet red pepper (about 2 large peppers)	¾ cup sugar
	½ cup cider vinegar
1½ tsp. salt	1 8-ounce wheel Camembert

◆ In a bowl, combine chopped peppers and salt. Let stand for 2 to 3 hours.

◆ Drain peppers in a colander. Transfer to a medium saucepan. Add sugar and vinegar.

◆ Cook over low heat until syrup has thickened and skins on peppers are tender. (About 1 hour). Let cool.

◆ Trim rind from chilled Camembert with a sharp knife. Bring to room temperature.

◆ Before serving, place Camembert on an ovenproof plate or shallow baking dish. Drain excess liquid from the relish and spread the relish over the top of the Camembert. Bake at 275° for 15 minutes, or until the Camembert is melted. Spread on crackers to serve.

 Grub Club Tip
You may substitute Brie for the Camembert.

Cocktail
Champagne is a classic symbol of celebration and good taste. From the popping of the cork, to the moment the bubbles tickle your nose, to the palate-tingling first sip, you know you're part of something special. Choose a good champagne and serve in flutes, as is, or with a splash of Crème de Cassis for a Kir Royale.

◆ ACT II ◆

TOSSED SALAD ELEGANTE

Cool, crisp, and classic.

½ head Boston or butter lettuce, torn into bite-size pieces

1 small bunch romaine lettuce, torn into bite-size pieces

1½ cups sliced fresh mushrooms

1 medium leek, thinly sliced

½ pound cooked medium shrimp

½ cup freshly grated Parmesan cheese

Dijon Vinaigrette

¼ cup extra-virgin olive oil

2 Tbsp. red wine vinegar

1 Tbsp. grated Parmesan cheese

1 Tbsp. Dijon mustard

¼ tsp. salt

¼ tsp. ground white pepper

◆ Shake dressing ingredients in a tightly covered container. Refrigerate for at least one hour.

◆ Just before serving, toss lettuces, mushrooms, and leeks with dressing. Arrange on individual salad plates. Top each serving with shrimp, French bread croutons (recipe follows) and a sprinkling of freshly grated Parmesan cheese.

FRENCH BREAD CROUTONS

4 slices French bread, each ½-inch thick

1 Tbsp. olive oil

2 large cloves garlic, cut length-wise into halves

◆ Tear bread into ½-inch pieces.

◆ Sauté garlic in olive oil in a small skillet over medium heat until golden. Remove garlic and discard.

◆ Add bread to oil. Cook and stir until bread is golden brown. Remove from heat and spread on paper towels to cool. Store in an airtight container until ready to use.

Wine
An Italian dry white wine, such as an Orvieto Classico or a Vernaccia would be just right with the salad.

◆ ACT III ◆

BAKED CHICKEN WITH POACHED ORANGES

An exceptionally elegant presentation, with gorgeous color and a heavenly aroma. This is among the many wonderful recipes that Grub Club member Nick Prebezac has created for our enjoyment.

8 boneless chicken breast halves, with skin
1 tsp. salt
1 Tbsp. crushed basil
½ tsp. ground ginger
½ tsp. white pepper
½ cup ketchup
½ cup soy sauce
¼ cup vegetable oil
¼ cup honey

1 Tbsp. Grand Marnier liqueur
2 cloves garlic, crushed
4 cups hot, cooked rice

Poached Oranges
¾ cup water
1½ cups sugar
3 oranges
3 Tbsp. slivered orange peel
1 Tbsp. Grand Marnier liqueur

◆ Preheat oven to 350°.

◆ Arrange chicken pieces in a shallow baking pan. Combine salt, crushed basil, ground ginger, and white pepper. Sprinkle over chicken.

◆ Mix together ketchup, soy sauce, vegetable oil, honey, 1 tablespoon Grand Marnier, and garlic. Baste chicken pieces with sauce. Place in oven and bake for 1 hour, basting occasionally, until chicken is tender.

◆ While chicken is baking, combine water, sugar, and slivered orange peel in a small saucepan. Bring to a boil. Reduce heat and simmer until syrup has thickened, about 20 minutes.

◆ Peel and section the oranges. Remove white membrane. Cut each section into 3 or 4 pieces with a sharp knife. Add orange pieces and 1 tablespoon Grand Marnier to simmering syrup. Poach for 3 minutes.

◆ Drain oranges, reserving syrup. Combine reserved syrup with remaining basting sauce in a small saucepan. Cook over medium heat until sauce has thickened slightly.

◆ Serve chicken with rice and poached oranges on the side. Drizzle chicken and rice with the sauce.

JULIENNED CARROTS WITH THYME

Subtle and sophisticated.

6 small carrots, peeled and cut into matchstick-sized pieces

4 Tbsp. butter, cut into pieces

½ tsp. ground thyme

Dash salt

Fresh thyme or parsley sprigs for garnish

◆ Place carrots in a medium saucepan with water to cover. Bring to a boil. Lower heat and cover. Cook for 10 minutes, or until tender.

◆ Drain carrots and return to low heat. Add butter, thyme, and salt. Stir gently until butter is melted and carrots are well coated. Remove from heat. Garnish with sprigs of fresh thyme or parsley.

Wine

Serve an Oregon or California Pinot Noir, or a Beaujolais-Villages with this course.

◆ ACT IV ◆

CHOCOLATE MINT MOUSSE

Divine decadence—a chocolate lover's fantasy, with the rich, refreshing flavor of an after-dinner mint.

8 ounces semi-sweet chocolate	1 cup whipping cream
⅓ cup boiling water	¼ cup confectioners sugar
5 large eggs, separated	½ tsp. vanilla extract
½ tsp. peppermint extract	Shaved chocolate (optional)
Pinch of salt	Small sprigs of fresh mint (optional)

◆ Coarsely chop chocolate and place in the top of a double boiler set over simmering water. Pour in the boiling water. Stir until melted and smooth. Remove from heat and allow to cool for about 5 minutes.

◆ In a medium bowl, beat the egg yolks with an electric mixer for 3 to 4 minutes until they are thick and lemon-colored.

◆ Reduce speed to low; gradually add chocolate and then the peppermint extract and beat just until blended and smooth. (Taste mixture at this point. If it is not "minty" enough, add an extra drop or two of extract).

◆ Clean beaters well. In another bowl, beat egg whites with pinch of salt only until they hold a definite shape, but not until they are stiff and dry.

◆ Gently fold about one-quarter of the beaten egg whites into the chocolate mixture, then fold in the second quarter. Finally, fold the chocolate into the remaining egg whites, folding only until no white streaks remain.

◆ Transfer the mousse to a decorative serving bowl, or individual dessert dishes or stemmed glasses. Cover with plastic wrap and refrigerate for at least 3 hours or overnight.

◆ Before serving, softly whip the cream with the confectioners sugar and vanilla extract. Top each serving of mousse with whipped cream and garnish with optional shaved chocolate and/or fresh mint sprigs.

Coffee

Cups of frothy cappuccino, served with slivers of lemon peel, make any occasion special. Or, serve a premium-quality coffee, dressed up with softly whipped cream.

Curtain Call

A sip of fine cognac or brandy is the perfect finale to your Elegant Interlude.

NOTES

_____

_____

_____

_____

_____

_____

_____

_____

_____

_____

_____

_____

_____

_____

_____

_____

_____

Irish Supper

Act I

Shamrock Dip

Lucky Potato Skins

Irish Beer

◆

Act II

Colcannon Soup

Irish Soda Bread

Irish Beer

◆

Act III

Kelli's Irish Stew

Irish Soda Bread

Guinness Stout

◆

Act IV

Apple Cake with Lemon Custard Sauce

Irish Coffee

Bailey's Irish Cream or Irish Mist

◆ IRISH SUPPER ◆

The folklore of Ireland is rich with romance and whimsy—limericks and leprechauns, and tales of kissing the blarney stone for luck. The enduring pride of the Irish people and those of Irish descent is evidenced in the celebration of St. Patrick's Day. It's a day when "everyone is Irish," a holiday that is warmly embraced by people of all nationalities and ancestry.

The cuisine of the Emerald Isle is simple, honest, and substantial, based on such humble ingredients as potatoes and cabbage. It is uncomplicated to prepare and easy to enjoy. Our "Irish Supper" nourishes the body and soul with dishes that have satisfied for centuries.

What better way to chase away the chill of a blustery winter day than with a bowl of hearty Irish Stew, washed down with a sturdy ale? What more perfect way to celebrate a beloved holiday?

Decor

If you are the lucky owner of such Irish treasures as Waterford crystal, Beleek china, or some lovely Irish linens and laces, they would be perfectly at home at your "Irish Supper." Perhaps you prefer to play up the party atmosphere of a traditional St. Patrick's Day celebration, with shamrock cut-outs, bright green streamers, party hats, and balloons. Your local party supply store will have a wealth of props to choose from, including humorous cocktail napkins and coasters to serve along with your Irish beers and ales.

Attire

Hand-knit sweaters, woolen tweeds, and wool caps are traditional Irish garb. Be sure to wear something green, and don't forget your "Kiss Me, I'm Irish" button.

Music

You'll find plenty of variety in Irish music, from traditional Irish folk songs, to lilting ballads such as "Danny Boy" sung in rich Irish tenors, to rollicking Irish drinking songs.

Activities

The Irish people love to make toasts celebrating the friendship and goodwill they share with their friends. Have each party member compose a toast, and then present it during the event when the spirit moves them. Toasts can be humorous or sentimental, or a little of both. If you prefer, purchase a book of Irish toasts to pass around and have everyone read their favorite. Here is an example to get you started.

"May the roof above us never fall in, and may the friends gathered below never fall out."

◆ ACT I ◆

SHAMROCK DIP

As festive as a four-leaf clover!

1 10-ounce package frozen chopped spinach

¼ cup chopped green onions (including tops)

½ cup lightly packed parsley sprigs

2 cloves garlic, chopped

1 cup sour cream

1 tsp. pepper

⅛ tsp. celery seed

Salt to taste

◆ Thaw spinach and drain well. Squeeze out as much liquid as possible.

◆ Place spinach along with other ingredients (except for salt) in the container of a food processor or blender. Whirl until blended and fairly smooth.

◆ Transfer to small bowl. Salt to taste. Cover and refrigerate for at least 2 hours, or overnight.

◆ Serve with green pepper strips, turnip slices, and/or potato chips.

LUCKY POTATO SKINS

A great way to enjoy Ireland's favorite vegetable.

8 large russet potatoes

¼ cup olive oil

½ cup melted butter

2 cups grated extra-sharp cheddar cheese

1 cup grated Monterey Jack cheese

1 cup sliced black olives

6-8 green onions, thinly sliced

◆ Scrub potatoes and pierce each in several places with a fork. Place in a large baking pan and brush lightly with olive oil.

◆ Bake in a 400° oven for 1 hour, or until soft when pressed. Remove from oven. Let stand until cool enough to handle.

◆ Cut each potato lengthwise into quarters. With a spoon, scoop out flesh, leaving a ⅛-inch-thick shell. (Reserve flesh for other uses.)

◆ Brush skins inside and out with melted butter. Arrange skin side down on a broiling pan. Broil at 450° for 3 to 5 minutes.

◆ Remove from oven. Sprinkle evenly with grated cheeses and olives. Broil until cheese is melted, about 2 to 4 minutes. Sprinkle with sliced green onions.

Cocktail

Irish beer goes best with Irish food. Try Harp's Lager, a rich and flavorful ale.

◆ Act II ◆

COLCANNON SOUP

Traditionally, Colcannon is a dish made from mashed potatoes and cabbage. Here, the ingredients are puréed into a smooth, creamy soup and garnished with bacon and onions for extra flavor.

2 cups water

2 14-ounce cans chicken broth

4 cups peeled, coarsely chopped baking potato (about 2 medium potatoes)

5 cups coarsely shredded green cabbage

1 medium onion, chopped

¾ cup half-and-half

½ tsp. salt

¼ tsp. pepper

½ pound bacon, diced

⅓ cup sliced green onion tops

◆ In a small frying pan, sauté bacon until crisp. Drain on paper towels and set aside.

◆ In a large saucepan or Dutch oven, bring water and broth to a boil. Add chopped potato. Reduce heat, cover, and simmer for 20 minutes.

◆ Add cabbage and onion. Cover and simmer for 30 minutes or until tender.

◆ Remove from heat. In a blender, purée soup in batches and return to pan. Return pan to heat. Stir in salt, pepper, and half-and-half. Cook over low heat until thoroughly heated.

◆ Serve in large mugs, topped with a sprinkling of bacon and sliced green onion tops.

 ### Grub Club Tip
Soup may be made ahead and gently reheated.

IRISH SODA BREAD

I'm always on the lookout for good breads that don't take a lot of time or work to make. This bread fits the bill nicely. Though it is typically Irish, it could be served with just about any soup or stew.

6 cups flour	3 Tbsp. cornstarch
2 tsp. sugar	1 tsp. salt
2 tsp. baking powder	2½ cups buttermilk
2 tsp. baking soda	

◆ Preheat oven to 375°.

◆ In a large bowl, combine dry ingredients. Pour in buttermilk and mix until a soft dough is formed.

◆ Transfer dough to a lightly floured surface. Knead until dough is well mixed and fairly smooth, about 1 minute.

◆ Divide dough in half and shape each half into a round, slightly flattened loaf. Place the two loaves on an ungreased baking sheet. With a sharp knife, cut long, ½-inch-deep slashes in a cross shape on the top of each loaf. Allow the bread to rest for 15 minutes.

◆ Bake for 35 to 40 minutes until golden brown. Cool. Just before serving, cut each loaf into 8 wedges.

Grub Club Tip

Since this recipe makes two loaves of bread, you will have a loaf to serve with the Colcannon Soup and another to serve with Kelli's Irish Stew in Act III.

Beverage

Continue with beer, either the Harp's Lager or another Irish brew of your choice. Wine-lovers might appreciate a dry white wine such as a Pinot Blanc.

◆ ACT III ◆

KELLI'S IRISH STEW

Grub Club member Kelli Keaton Ambrosi drew from her Irish heritage to create a stew we all would love.

3 Tbsp. vegetable oil

3 pounds beef stew meat, cut into 1½-inch cubes

2 large yellow onions, peeled and cut into ¼-inch slices

4 cloves garlic, chopped

2 tsp. dried thyme

2 tsp. dried rosemary, crushed

¼ cup flour

1 14-ounce can beef broth

1 cup Guinness stout

6 medium potatoes, peeled and cut into chunks

1 pound carrots, cut into 1-inch pieces

3 bay leaves

Salt and pepper to taste

◆ In a Dutch oven, heat the vegetable oil over medium heat. Add meat and brown on all sides.

◆ Add the onion and garlic. Cook until the onion is translucent.

◆ Reduce heat to low. Add flour, thyme, and rosemary. Stir until thoroughly blended.

◆ Stir in beef broth and Guinness stout. Simmer, stirring, until mixture thickens slightly.

◆ Add potatoes, carrots, and bay leaves. Cover and simmer for 1½ hours or until vegetables and meat are tender. Season to taste with salt and pepper before serving.

Beverage

Serve Guinness stout—a dark, rich Irish brew with lots of body and flavor. If you prefer wine, we suggest an Oregon Pinot Noir.

◆ ACT IV ◆

APPLE CAKE WITH LEMON CUSTARD SAUCE

A moist, lemony cake studded with apples and raisins, and topped with a creamy custard.

¾ cup butter, softened
½ cup sugar
3 eggs
Grated zest of 1 lemon
3 medium apples, pared, cored, and diced
Juice of ½ lemon

¼ cup golden raisins
1½ cups sifted cake flour
1½ tsp. double-acting baking powder
¼ tsp. salt
⅛ tsp. nutmeg

◆ Preheat oven to 375°. Grease an 8 x 8 x 2-inch baking dish.

◆ Toss diced apples with lemon juice. Set aside.

◆ In a large bowl, beat butter and sugar with an electric mixer on medium speed until creamy. Beat in eggs one at a time. Stir in diced apples, raisins, and lemon zest.

◆ Sift together flour, baking powder, and salt. Stir in nutmeg. Fold into butter mixture until well blended.

◆ Spread into baking dish. Bake 30 to 35 minutes until golden and a tooth-pick inserted into center comes out clean.

◆ Cool and cut into squares. Top each serving with Lemon Custard Sauce. (Recipe on following page).

Lemon Custard Sauce

½ cup sugar	1 cup warm water
1½ Tbsp. cornstarch	2 egg yolks, beaten
Pinch salt	2 Tbsp. melted butter
Pinch nutmeg	2 Tbsp. fresh lemon juice

◆ In a non-aluminum saucepan, combine sugar, cornstarch, salt, and nutmeg. Slowly stir in the water. Cook over medium-high heat, stirring constantly, until sauce thickens.

◆ Whisk one-half cup of the heated sauce into the beaten egg yolks. Stir the mixture back into the saucepan. Cook and stir for 1 minute more.

◆ Remove from heat and blend in the butter and lemon juice. Cool, and chill until serving.

Coffee

No Irish celebration would be complete without Irish coffee, served in hefty mugs. Place a teaspoon of sugar into each mug. Add enough hot, strong coffee to dissolve sugar and stir. Add a jigger of Irish whiskey to each mug, then fill mug with more coffee. Top with softly whipped cream. Do not stir.

Curtain Call

For a final toast, serve delicious Bailey's Irish Cream, or Irish Mist—an Irish whiskey-based liqueur flavored with honey and a little orange.

◆ ◆ ◆
Spring Fling

Act I

Orange Currant Scones

Raspberry Butter

Mimosas

◆

Act II

*Chilled Strawberry Melon Soup
with Gingered Melon Balls*

Berry Seltzer

◆

Act III

Golden Brunch Strata

Garden Sunshine Salad

Orange Juice or Lemonade

◆

Act IV

Fruit Fantasy Parfaits

Fruit Spritzers

◆ Spring Fling ◆

*W*ho can resist the spell of springtime? Our spirits soar as we watch the days grow longer, the weather warmer, and the landscape around us burst into bud and bloom. Suddenly we are suffused with energy as we launch into spring cleaning and gardening, as we pack away our woolen sweaters and bring out our lawn chairs, eager to welcome the new and glorious season.

Such a time of hope and renewal is cause for a special kind of celebration. As a fitting change of pace, our Spring Fling is a brunch. An early, leisurely meal leaves the afternoon free for the multitude of springtime activities that beckon.

This is your prescription for shaking off winter's mental cobwebs; all those other chores can wait. For now, your only responsibility is to enjoy the company of your friends, and of Mother Nature at her finest.

Decor

Perfection would be dining alfresco on your deck or patio. If it's still just a bit too cool or if spring showers threaten, dining inside can be every bit as festive. A profusion of pastels will make your table look fresh and spring-like; flowers and greenery are essential. Cut tulips and daffodils can provide a happy splash of color. Small pots of primroses or crocus can be enjoyed all season, or sent home with guests.

Baskets of pastel-dyed eggs are an attractive addition to a springtime table. Use flower pots to hold napkins and flatware. Other props to consider are decorative birdhouses, watering cans, and gardening tools.

Attire

Make your guests part of the decor—ask everyone to wear pastels. If your activities are garden related, gardening clothes would be appropriate and fun.

Music

George Winston's "Winter Into Spring" collection of piano solos on the Windham Hill label is a lovely tribute to the changing of the seasons, and a pleasant background to your spring brunch.

Activities

Choose your activities based on the weather and the passions of your group. An excursion to a nearby park or arboretum would be perfect for a balmy spring day. If your group loves to garden, have an exchange of seeds, starts, and bulbs, or take a trip together to a local nursery to stock up. Organize an Easter egg dyeing session, or have a grown-up Easter egg hunt, indoors or out, complete with prizes. If your group is feeling particularly frisky, go fly a kite!

◆ ACT I ◆

ORANGE CURRANT SCONES

A kiss of orange makes ordinary scones extraordinary.

2 cups flour	1 Tbsp. grated orange zest
2 Tbsp. sugar	6 Tbsp. butter, softened
1 Tbsp. baking powder	½ cup milk
½ tsp. salt	1 egg, lightly beaten
¾ cup currants	

◆ Preheat oven to 400°.

◆ In a large bowl, combine flour, sugar, baking powder, and salt. Stir in orange zest and currants.

◆ Cut in butter until mixture is crumbly. Add egg and milk and stir until dough clings together.

◆ Knead gently (about 12 times) on a lightly floured board. Cut dough into fourths and form each fourth into a ½-inch-thick square. Cut each square diagonally twice to form 4 triangles.

◆ Place triangles on a lightly greased baking sheet and bake for 15 to 20 minutes, until golden brown.

Grub Club Tip

Make scones the morning of the event. While still warm, wrap in a towel to transport to your host's house.

Raspberry Butter

A fresh and fruity spread for scones, muffins, waffles, or any breakfast treat. This may also be made with fresh or frozen strawberries.

½ cup (1 stick) unsalted butter, softened

¼ cup confectioners sugar

1 cup fresh raspberries, or thawed and drained frozen raspberries

◆ With an electric mixer or food processor, whip together butter and sugar until fluffy. Add raspberries and continue beating until blended and smooth. Makes about 1 cup.

Y Cocktail

Celebrate spring with sparkling Mimosas. Fill champagne flutes with half orange juice and half chilled champagne. Stir gently.

Grub Club Tip

Act I on its own makes a perfect breakfast in bed.

◆ ACT II ◆

CHILLED STRAWBERRY MELON SOUP
WITH GINGERED MELON BALLS

A very pretty presentation—creamy smooth and delightfully refreshing.

½ cup unsweetened pineapple juice

⅓ cup sugar

1 Tbsp. grated fresh ginger

2 small cantaloupes

½ small honeydew melon

3 cups fresh strawberries, or frozen unsweetened strawberries, thawed

1 8-ounce container plain yogurt

¼ tsp. vanilla

1 8-ounce container sour cream

1 cup half-and-half

Mint leaves for garnish (optional)

◆ In a small saucepan, combine the pineapple juice, sugar, and ginger. Bring to a boil, stirring until sugar is dissolved. Reduce heat and simmer for 5 to 7 minutes until mixture has the consistency of a thin syrup. Remove from heat and cool.

◆ With a melon-baller, scoop out 4 cups of cantaloupe balls and 2 cups of honeydew balls. Place melon balls in a storage container and toss gently with ginger syrup. Cover and refrigerate overnight.

◆ Scoop remaining cantaloupe from rind and set aside.

◆ In a blender or food processor, purée the strawberries. Remove and set aside. Purée the reserved cantaloupe.

◆ In a large bowl, stir together the yogurt, sour cream, and vanilla. Add puréed strawberries, melon, and half-and-half and stir until blended. Cover and chill overnight.

◆ To serve, drain melon balls and stir syrup into chilled soup. Ladle soup into bowls. Top with melon balls. If desired, garnish with fresh mint leaves.

Beverage

A glass of clear berry-flavored seltzer served over ice and garnished with a perfect ripe strawberry would be light and refreshing.

◆ Act III ◆

GOLDEN BRUNCH STRATA

Layers of savory ingredients topped with Cheddar cheese and baked until golden. Assemble the night before, and in the morning, simply pop into the oven.

1 medium onion, chopped

½ pound fresh mushrooms, sliced

1 Tbsp. vegetable oil

2 Tbsp. dry sherry

16 slices stale white bread, crusts removed

¼ pound Canadian bacon or ham, diced

16 slices Cheddar cheese

6 eggs

½ tsp. each salt, pepper, and dry mustard

2 tsp. Worcestershire sauce

2½ cups whole milk

2 cups grated Cheddar cheese

2 Tbsp. snipped fresh chives

◆ In a medium skillet, sauté the onions in the vegetable oil until translucent. Add mushrooms and sherry and sauté for 2 to 3 minutes. Remove onions and mushrooms from pan with a slotted spoon and set aside to cool slightly.

◆ Butter a 9 x 13-inch glass baking dish. Place half of the bread slices in the bottom of the dish. Spoon onion/mushroom mixture over bread and sprinkle with diced Canadian bacon or ham. Arrange slices of cheese in a layer, and top with remaining bread slices. Press down lightly to compact.

◆ In a medium bowl, beat eggs with salt, pepper, and dry mustard. Add milk and Worcestershire sauce. Whisk until thoroughly blended. Pour egg mixture over assembled layers. Cover and refrigerate overnight.

◆ The next day, preheat oven to 325°. Sprinkle grated Cheddar cheese over top. Bake, uncovered for 45 minutes to 1 hour, until golden and bubbly.

◆ Remove from oven and let stand for 10 minutes. Sprinkle with snipped chives. Cut into squares and serve.

GARDEN SUNSHINE SALAD

Yellow peppers and a lemony dressing make this crunchy salad a perfect addition to a spring menu.

1 pound fresh green beans, ends trimmed (or frozen beans, thawed and drained)

2 sweet yellow peppers, seeded and julienned

½ pound jicama, peeled and julienned

Dressing

¼ cup fresh lemon juice

1 tsp. Dijon mustard

1 tsp. finely chopped chives

½ cup olive oil

Salt and pepper to taste

◆ In a medium saucepan, bring water to a boil. Add green beans and cook for 7 to 10 minutes. (Beans should remain slightly crisp). Drain and plunge into ice water to stop the cooking.

◆ Drain beans in a colander. Combine with peppers and jicama.

◆ To make dressing, combine lemon juice, mustard, and chives in a small bowl. Slowly pour in olive oil, whisking constantly until thoroughly blended. Season to taste with salt and pepper.

◆ Toss vegetables with dressing. Cover and refrigerate several hours or overnight.

Grub Club Tip
Jicama is a root vegetable with a bark-like skin and white, juicy, slightly sweet flesh with a texture somewhat like a radish. It can be used in place of water chestnuts or apples (it doesn't discolor when exposed to air) in salads or any dish where you want a bit of refreshing crunch.

Beverage
Serve frosty glasses of orange juice or lemonade, garnished with citrus wedges.

◆ ACT IV ◆

FRUIT FANTASY PARFAITS

Light enough for a brunch, yet special enough to serve any time. Purchase the fresh fruit 2 or 3 days before the event to allow time to ripen.

½ cup sliced almonds

½ cup flaked coconut

¼ cup golden raisins

4 medium peaches or nectarines

4 medium plums

2 cups strawberries

1 12-ounce package frozen
blueberries, thawed and drained

¼ cup Amaretto

2 cups plain yogurt

1 cup sour cream

2 Tbsp. honey

1 tsp. vanilla

¼ tsp. almond extract

◆ In a small skillet, toast the almonds and coconut over medium heat, stirring constantly, until the coconut is golden, about 5 to 6 minutes. Set aside to cool, then stir in raisins.

◆ Slice the strawberries. Cut up the peaches and plums into bite-size pieces. Combine with blueberries in a medium bowl. Toss with the Amaretto.

◆ In a small bowl, blend yogurt, sour cream, honey, vanilla, and almond extract.

◆ Layer the fruit and yogurt mixture into parfait or other tall glasses, adding 1 Tbsp. of the coconut mixture to each glass when it is half filled. Top the parfaits with the remaining coconut mixture.

Grub Club Tip
Parfaits may be assembled ahead of time (coconut mixture will lose some of its crunch) or at the host's house just before serving.

Coffee
Coffee should be available throughout the brunch. Keep brewed coffee hot and fresh in a thermos or thermal carafe. Tea drinkers might enjoy a lemon-mint blend, served with thin wedges of lemon.

•   •   •   •   •   •   •   •   •   •   •

🍷 Curtain Call

It is unlikely that you will be serving a liqueur at a brunch. However, if you hold your event in the evening (the menu works beautifully as a light dinner) serve fruit spritzers. Pour a shot of fruit liqueur, such as peach, melon, or raspberry, over a glass of ice and add a splash of club soda or plain seltzer.

NOTES

_____

_____

_____

_____

_____

_____

_____

_____

_____

_____

_____

_____

_____

_____

_____

_____

_____

_____

_____

_____

◆ ◆ ◆
Taste of Thailand

Act I

Spring Rolls

———

Thai Dipping Sauce

———

Sake

◆

Act II

Pork Satay

———

Spicy Peanut Sauce

———

Singha Beer

◆

Act III

Sesame Chicken Stir-Fry

———

Steamed Rice

———

Singha Beer

◆

Act IV

Coconut Ice Cream with Mangoes

———

Thai Iced Coffee

———

Ginger Liqueur

◆ TASTE OF THAILAND ◆

*T*he popularity of Thai food in the United States is something of a phenomenon, and those of us who have discovered it are smitten. Thai food is a tantalizing mix of Chinese, Indian, and Southeast Asian cuisine, combining interesting textures and contrasting flavors—sweet, salty, and spicy—into a surprising array of dishes.

The unique appeal of Thai food can be attributed to its sauces, which are primarily a blend of peanuts, coconut milk, various curry pastes, and a potent smelling "fish sauce." Garlic, ginger, and coriander are the traditional flavorings, along with lemon grass and chili peppers. Look for these ingredients in an Oriental grocery. Some may be available in the ethnic food section of your supermarket.

As in most of Asia, rice is a staple. In fact, the Thai phrase "gin khow," which is used to say "let's eat" translates literally as "eat rice." Much of the cooking is done in a wok, and food is eaten with traditional silverware, with the exception of noodle dishes, which are eaten with chopsticks. Since we enjoy the novelty of eating with chopsticks and look for opportunities to use them, we forgo forks altogether at our Thai meals. Whatever utensils you decide to use, be prepared for a taste adventure. Gin khow!

Decor

Asian style has a beauty all its own that lends itself to gracious entertaining. Your table may be simply set with straw or bamboo mats, plain dishes, and cloth napkins folded into fans. Lay pairs of chopsticks across small, flat stones at each place setting. For your centerpiece, fill a graceful bowl with water and float candles or a few exotic blossoms. Lighting should be tranquil. Oriental shoji screens surrounding your dining area can heighten the sense of intimacy.

Our hosts cut bamboo branches from their back yard, sprayed them with metallic gold paint, and arranged them in tall vases. Bare tree branches with sculptural qualities would be equally stunning. Oriental grocery stores and import stores sell inexpensive props such as paper fans and parasols that can add extra Oriental flavor to your Thai experience, and may be brought out and enjoyed any time you entertain with Asian cuisine.

Attire

Thailand is famous for its sumptuous silks and distinctive prints. Choose clothing in rich, jewellike colors, and embellish with gold accents.

Music

Check your library for music from Thailand. If it is difficult to find, other Oriental melodies will suffice.

Activities

Movie buffs might enjoy a private showing of "The King and I," with Yul Brynner as the king of Siam (Thailand's former name) and Deborah Kerr as a British schoolteacher who is hired to tutor his children. Lots of atmosphere!

◆ ACT I ◆

SPRING ROLLS

A favorite Oriental hor d'oeuvre.

¼ pound mushrooms

1 small red bell pepper, cored, seeded, and cut into pieces

½ cup chopped celery

3 green onions, including tops, cut into pieces

3 cloves garlic

1 Tbsp. chopped fresh coriander (cilantro)

2 tsp. sesame oil

Dash hot pepper oil (optional)

½ pound chopped cooked shrimp

½ tsp. curry powder

¼ tsp. ground ginger

1 tsp. soy sauce

1 16-ounce package egg roll wrappers

3 or 4 Nappa cabbage leaves, shredded

1 cup bean sprouts

Paste of 2 Tbsp. flour plus 1 tsp. water

Peanut oil

◆ In a food processor, finely chop the mushrooms, red bell pepper, celery, green onions, garlic, and coriander.

◆ In a wok or stir-fry pan, heat the sesame oil and hot pepper oil over medium-high heat. Add the chopped vegetables. Stir-fry for 1 minute. Add the chopped shrimp, curry powder, ginger, and soy sauce. Stir-fry for 1 minute more. Remove mixture from wok and set aside to cool. Clean wok.

◆ To assemble spring rolls, place a few shreds of Nappa cabbage in the middle of an egg roll wrapper. Top with a tablespoon of the stir-fried vegetable mixture and a few bean sprouts. Roll up diagonally, tucking in ends to form a "package." Seal end with a small dab of flour-water paste.

◆ Continue with remaining ingredients until filling is used up. (You should end up with about 16 Spring Rolls).

◆ Heat about 1-inch of peanut oil in the wok over medium-high heat. Fry 3 or 4 Spring Rolls at a time for 3 or 4 minutes until golden. Drain on paper towels. Serve with Thai Dipping Sauce. (Recipe follows).

 Grub Club Tip
The Spring Rolls may be kept warm or reheated in a 300° oven.

THAI DIPPING SAUCE

1 cup ketchup

3 cloves garlic, crushed

1 tsp. grated fresh ginger

2 tsp. soy sauce

2 tsp. lime juice

◆ Combine all ingredients in a small bowl. Serve at room temperature as a dipping sauce with the Spring Rolls.

Cocktail
Sake, an Oriental rice wine, has an intriguing flavor that is worth experiencing. Serve in small glasses, or purchase an inexpensive sake serving set at your local Oriental grocery or import store. Depending on the variety, sake may be served hot, at room temperature, or chilled. Try several different varieties, available in small bottles.

◆ ACT II ◆

PORK SATAY

This dish shows up at a lot of our parties. Strips of meat (pork, beef, and chicken are all good) are marinated in a curry-coconut milk mixture, and then skewered and grilled and served with a spicy peanut sauce for dipping.

1 14-ounce can unsweetened coconut milk

1 Tbsp. Thai red curry paste

1 Tbsp. fish sauce

1 Tbsp. curry powder

2 pounds pork tenderloin, sliced into thin strips, about 1 x 3 inches

12-inch bamboo skewers, soaked in water for 1-2 hours

◆ In a 9 x 13-inch glass baking dish, blend the coconut milk, curry paste, fish sauce, and curry powder until smooth. Add pork strips and stir to cover. Refrigerate at least 6 hours, or overnight.

◆ Preheat oven broiler or outdoor grill. Weave 2 strips of pork lengthwise onto each skewer. Broil or grill for 5 minutes on each side. Serve with Spicy Peanut Sauce. (Recipe follows).

Grub Club Tip
Thai red curry paste is a blend of dried red chilies, garlic, and spices, and is available in jars. Fish sauce is a thin, salty brown liquid. Don't be put off by its strong aroma—it mellows significantly upon cooking.

Spicy Peanut Sauce

This sauce is so good that we often make a double batch. We use the leftovers as a pasta sauce (toss a spoonful with hot vermicelli or spaghetti) or as a dip with Chinese pea pods and other crudités.

1 14-ounce can unsweetened coconut milk

1 Tbsp. Thai red curry paste

½ cup peanut butter (smooth or crunchy)

2 Tbsp. sugar

2 Tbsp. rice vinegar

1 Tbsp. fish sauce

◆ Stir the coconut milk until smooth. Heat half of the coconut milk in a saucepan. Add the red curry paste and stir until mixture is thoroughly blended and turns a pale amber color.

◆ Blend in the peanut butter, sugar, vinegar, fish sauce, and remaining coconut milk. Cook for 8 to 10 minutes, stirring frequently, until sauce has thickened slightly.

◆ Remove from heat and allow to cool.

Grub Club Tip

The sauce may be prepared in advance and gently reheated before serving until just warm. It will keep in the refrigerator for about a week.

Beverage

The spicy flavors of Thai food are best served with a robust beer or ale. Singha Beer, which is actually a malt liquor brewed in Thailand, is the perfect complement to Thai dishes.

◆ ACT III ◆

SESAME CHICKEN STIR-FRY

This colorful and tasty dish is full of interesting Oriental vegetables. For best results, serve immediately, right from the wok, while the vegetables are hot and crisp.

1 cup dried Oriental mushrooms (such as Shiitake)

½ cup flour

2 tsp. salt

2 tsp. ground black pepper

2 pounds boneless chicken breasts, cut into 1-inch strips

¼ cup peanut oil

¼ cup sesame oil

3 cloves garlic, minced

½ tsp. red pepper flakes

1 cup Nappa cabbage, cut into bite-size chunks

1 cup bok choy, stems and leaves, cut into bite-size pieces

1 medium red bell pepper, julienned

1 cup fresh snow pea pods, ends trimmed

¾ cup canned baby corn, halved lengthwise

¾ cup canned chicken broth

Juice from ½ lime

2 Tbsp. fish sauce

1 Tbsp. sugar

1½ Tbsp. arrowroot powder

Coriander (cilantro) leaves for garnish

◆ Soak the dried mushrooms in hot water to cover for 20 minutes, or until softened. Drain. Discard tough stems and slice tops into ½-inch strips.

◆ In a medium bowl, combine flour, salt, and pepper. Add chicken strips and toss to coat.

◆ Heat the peanut and sesame oils in a wok or large frying pan over medium-high heat. When the oil just begins to smoke, add the chicken pieces and stir-fry for 3 to 5 minutes until lightly browned. Remove chicken from wok with a slotted spoon and set aside.

◆ To the wok, add the garlic, red pepper flakes, mushrooms, Nappa cabbage, bok choy, and red bell pepper. Stir-fry quickly, coating all the vegetables.

◆ Add the snow pea pods and baby corn and stir-fry for another 2 to 3 minutes. Stir in the chicken broth, lime juice, fish sauce, and sugar. Simmer for 1 minute.

◆ Dissolve the arrowroot powder in ¼ cup hot water and stir into vegetables.

◆ Add reserved chicken to wok. Lower the heat to medium and simmer, stirring occasionally, for 5 to 7 minutes or until sauce thickens.

◆ Serve at once, garnished with coriander leaves.

Grub Club Tip

The key to successful stir-frying is to have all your ingredients prepared and close at hand before you begin cooking. Work with a partner if possible. One person can add ingredients to the wok as needed, while the other person keeps the stir-fry process moving, stirring continuously to prevent the ingredients from sticking and burning.

STEAMED RICE

Rice is a central element in Thai meals. There are several methods of preparation. If you prefer (though purists may disagree) you may use your favorite brand of packaged rice, and simply follow package directions. You may also purchase long-grain rice in bulk. This rice must be rinsed well and drained before cooking. An electric rice steamer gives good, consistent results, though is a bit of an extravagance if you do not make rice often. One conventional method for preparing rice is to place rice and water (1 part rice to 2 parts water) in a pot with a tight-fitting lid. Bring to a boil (uncovered), then lower the heat, cover, and simmer for 20 minutes until rice is tender and all the water has been absorbed. Let stand for 5 minutes, fluff with a fork, and serve.

Beverage

Continue with beer or ale for this course.

◆ ACT IV ◆

COCONUT ICE CREAM WITH MANGOES

This deliciously different, not-too-sweet ice cream is one of the reasons we love eating out in Thai restaurants. We were delighted to discover that we could duplicate it at home.

1 14-ounce can unsweetened coconut milk

1 pint whipping cream

1 cup sugar

⅛ tsp. salt

1 large, firm-ripe mango, peeled, seeded, and diced

◆ In a large bowl, combine the coconut milk, whipping cream, sugar, and salt. Blend until smooth.

◆ Transfer mixture to an ice cream maker (for best results) and freeze according to manufacturer's directions. Or, transfer the mixture to a pan or stainless steel bowl and freeze until almost set. Beat with an electric mixer on low speed and return to the freezer until completely set. Best made the night before, to allow ample time for freezing.

◆ Top each serving with diced mango.

Grub Club Tip

The Coconut Ice Cream may also be served in the traditional way, topped with crushed, unsalted peanuts and a spoonful of palm seeds, which are transparent, chewy seeds that are packed in syrup and are available in cans at Oriental grocery stores.

Coffee

To make Thai iced coffee, first brew a pot of coffee and let cool to lukewarm. Pour into tall glasses filled with ice, top with about an inch of sweetened condensed milk, and stir.

Curtain Call

If you love the flavor of ginger as much as we do, try serving Canton Delicate Ginger Liqueur, or a ginger brandy. An Oriental plum wine would be pleasing as well.

NOTES

◆ ◆ ◆
Nifty Fifties

Act I

Peppy Party Mix

Perky Party Pinwheels

Sparkling Pink Punch

◆

Act II

Molded Waldorf Salad

Bake-and-Serve Dinner Rolls

Riesling

◆

Act III

Super-Duper Meat Loaf

Deluxe Scalloped Potatoes

Green Beans Supreme

Young Italian Chianti

◆

Act IV

Lemon Meringue Pie

Muscat Blanc or Orange Muscat

◆ NIFTY FIFTIES ◆

A merica in the Fifties was a happy place, defined by idealism and family values. The American Dream was alive and well. The world moved at a different pace than our busy world today. It was a safer world. Doors were left unlocked and neighbors were neighborly. Even the food was simple and non-threatening.

In the Fifties, the "four basic food groups" were the law of the land. Food's sole purpose was to nourish and nurture. Today we call this food "comfort food," and our nostalgia for it is so great that restaurants featuring Fifties dishes are a thriving business. Is it because of what the food stands for, or because it just plain tastes good? Perhaps it's a little of both.

Fifties families loved to entertain, and the "potluck" became a way of life. Books on entertaining gave hostesses tips on how to turn their favorite convenience foods into festive party fare. But the Baby Boomers have all grown up, and we couldn't resist adding a few of our own contemporary touches to our Nifty Fifties menu, such as Italian sausage in the meat loaf, and garlic in the green beans. We're pretty sure Ward and June would approve.

Creative Theme Parties

Decor

Fifties hostesses took their party-planning seriously, as entertaining was one of the few ways available for a woman to express her creativity. Table settings at dinner parties were carefully coordinated—the tablecloth matched the floral arrangement, which matched the candles, etc. Accessories such as paper lace doilies provided personality. Nothing too avant-garde, but always gracious and comfortable.

Attire

Men should strive for the "Ward Cleaver" look—shirt and tie, cardigan sweater, perhaps a pipe and Dad's old fedora. Ladies might plan a trip to the thrift store or Mom's attic for sweeping "June Cleaver" dresses, hats and gloves, stockings with seams, and a bib apron for time spent in the kitchen. Pumps and pearls and perfectly coiffed "do's," plus your reddest lipstick add more Fifties flair.

Music

Fifties music is easy to come by. Used record stores or Mom and Dad's collection (perhaps even your own?) will surely have a Frank Sinatra or Bing Crosby album, as well as songs by other famous crooners from this era. Throw in a little Elvis, and your bases are covered.

Activities

The Nifty Fifties have been captured forever in the TV shows that many of us grew up watching. Baby Boomers will fondly recall the refrain, "Hi, Honey, I'm home!" always followed by a cheerful and immaculate housewife greeting her husband at the door with a chaste kiss. Some of these classic shows are in syndication on cable channels, and could be taped for viewing at your Fifties affair. A round of charades, focusing on Fifties books, movies, TV shows, and songs would be a blast from the past and fun for all.

◆ ACT I ◆

PEPPY PARTY MIX

We forgot how addictive this stuff was! We munched so much that we almost ruined our appetites for dinner. Our version of this classic snack is a little peppier than the original, and calls for the addition of raisins and cashews because, well, we like them!

¼ cup butter or margarine

4 tsp. Worcestershire sauce

1 tsp. seasoned salt

¼ tsp. garlic powder

⅛ tsp. cayenne pepper

8 cups (any combination) corn, wheat, or rice cereal squares

½ cup salted (or honey-roasted) cashews

1 cup pretzel sticks

¾ cup raisins

◆ Preheat oven to 250°.

◆ In a roasting pan, melt butter in the oven. Stir in Worcestershire sauce, seasoned salt, garlic powder, and cayenne pepper.

◆ Gradually add cereal squares, cashews, pretzels, and raisins, stirring gently until ingredients are evenly coated.

◆ Bake 1 hour, stirring occasionally.

◆ Spread on paper towels to cool. Store in an airtight container.

PERKY PARTY PINWHEELS

Fifties hors d'oeuvre trays always seemed to include showy little tidbits like these.

1 8-ounce package cream cheese, softened

1 green onion, minced

¼ tsp. black pepper

¼ tsp. garlic powder

6 pieces thinly sliced boiled ham

24 pimento-stuffed green olives

Parsley for garnish

◆ In a small bowl, combine the softened cream cheese with the onion, pepper, and garlic powder.

◆ Spread the ham slices with the cream cheese mixture. Roll up, jelly-roll style. Cut into 1-inch pieces. Insert toothpicks (preferably frilled) crosswise into the ham rolls, then spear an olive crosswise onto each toothpick.

◆ Arrange the hors d'oeuvres in a starburst pattern on a serving platter. Garnish with plenty of fresh parsley sprigs.

SPARKLING PINK PUNCH

A party-perfect punch like this one looks Fifties-festive served in a punch bowl—the kind where the cups hook around the rim.

1 quart cranberry juice cocktail, chilled

1 6-ounce can frozen pink lemonade concentrate, thawed

1 quart sparkling water or plain seltzer, chilled

2 cups vodka (optional)

◆ In a punch bowl or other large bowl, combine the cranberry juice cocktail and the lemonade concentrate. Stir in the sparkling water or seltzer, and the optional vodka. Serve immediately.

Grub Club Tip

Make an ice ring mold with citrus slices or fresh strawberries to float in your punch.

◆ ACT II ◆

MOLDED WALDORF SALAD

The ubiquitous molded salad was guaranteed to show up on any Fifties buffet table. Gelatin offered limitless possibilities for creative expression. Here we've combined two Fifties standbys—the classic Waldorf Salad, plus fruit-flavored gelatin.

2 cups apple juice

1 3-ounce package lemon-flavored gelatin

1 cup finely chopped apple, tossed with 1 Tbsp. lemon juice

½ cup finely chopped walnuts

¼ cup finely chopped celery

1 small head Romaine lettuce

1 cup vanilla yogurt

◆ In a small saucepan, bring 1 cup of the apple juice to a boil. Dissolve gelatin in the boiling juice. Stir in the other cup of juice. Remove from heat.

◆ Transfer to a medium mixing bowl. Chill until mixture is the consistency of unbeaten egg whites.

◆ Fold in chopped apple, walnuts, and celery. Pour into a 3-cup mold or a glass bowl. Chill until completely set.

◆ Line individual salad plates with lettuce leaves. Stir vanilla yogurt until smooth.

◆ If using a mold, submerge mold in warm water to the rim for a few seconds, then invert onto a serving dish. Cut into pieces and arrange on salad plates. If using a bowl, simply spoon out individual servings onto plates.

◆ Top each serving with a spoonful of vanilla yogurt.

BREAD

Bake-and-serve dinner rolls—the kind that come in a cardboard tube in the dairy case of your grocery store—have been a boon to busy housewives for decades. Long before Americans discovered the pleasures of authentic, fresh-baked croissants and other esoteric foreign baked goods, we were enjoying crescent rolls, butterflake dinner rolls, and buttermilk biscuits right from our own ovens. Some of us even fought for the privilige of cracking open the tube on the edge of the kitchen counter! Try these again for a quick fix of nostalgia.

Wine

Our wine palates have evolved considerably since the Fifties, and our choices are infinitely more varied. Here you might try a late harvest Washington or California Riesling.

◆ ACT III ◆

SUPER-DUPER MEAT LOAF

One can hardly think about the Fifties without recalling meat loaf in its many guises. This version is as delicious as we remember, and special enough for company.

1½ pounds lean ground beef
½ pound mild Italian sausage
1 10-ounce package frozen chopped spinach, thawed, drained, and squeezed dry
1 medium onion, chopped
1½ cups soft bread crumbs
2 eggs, beaten
⅓ cup ketchup
2 Tbsp. Worcestershire sauce

1 tsp. salt
¼ tsp. pepper
½ cup grated mozzarella
⅓ cup grated Parmesan
¼ cup chopped fresh parsley

Topping
½ cup ketchup
½ cup grated mozzarella
¼ cup grated Parmesan

◆ Preheat oven to 350°.

◆ In a large bowl, combine ground beef, sausage, spinach, onion, bread crumbs, beaten eggs, ketchup, Worcestershire sauce, salt and pepper. Mix thoroughly.

◆ In a separate bowl combine grated mozzarella, Parmesan, and parsley.

◆ On a sheet of foil, spread the meat mixture into a rectangle, approximately 9 x 12-inches. Sprinkle cheese mixture on top to within ½-inch of edges.

◆ Grabbing edges of foil, fold over lengthwise. Peel back top of foil and press together edges and ends to form a loaf.

◆ Transfer to a 9 x 13-inch baking dish or pan. Bake for 45 minutes. Top with ketchup, then the ½ cup grated mozzarella and ¼ cup grated Parmesan. Continue baking for 15 more minutes or until done. Let stand 5 to 10 minutes before slicing.

Deluxe Scalloped Potatoes

Always welcome on a potluck buffet table, or alongside a hearty slice of meat loaf.

8 cups peeled, thinly sliced potatoes (about 8 medium potatoes)

¼ cup butter

¼ cup flour

1 tsp. salt

1 tsp. dry mustard

¼ tsp. pepper

2½ cups milk

3 cups shredded sharp cheddar cheese, divided

½ cup chopped onion

¼ cup chopped parsley

◆ Preheat oven to 350°.

◆ In a medium saucepan, melt butter over medium heat. Blend in flour, salt, dry mustard, and pepper.

◆ Gradually add milk. Cook, stirring constantly, until mixture thickens. Add 2 cups of the cheese and the chopped onion. Stir until the cheese is melted.

◆ In a 9 x 13-inch baking dish, layer potatoes and cheese sauce. Bake for 1 hour and 15 minutes or until potatoes are tender.

◆ Top with remaining cup of cheese and the parsley. Continue baking for 5 minutes or until cheese is melted.

Grub Club Tip

For extra tang, reduce the amount of cheddar cheese in the topping to ½ cup, and blend with ½ cup freshly grated Romano or Parmesan.

GREEN BEANS SUPREME

Back in the days when vegetables were canned, bland, and soggy, the command "eat your vegetables" seemed like punishment. In contrast, this crisp and flavorful dish is a treat.

1 medium onion, finely chopped	½ cup pitted ripe olives, chopped
4 cloves garlic, minced	1 ½ tsp. crushed dried oregano
2 Tbsp. olive oil	¾ tsp. lemon pepper
1 pound frozen whole green beans, thawed and drained	½ tsp. salt

◆ In a large skillet or stir-fry pan, heat olive oil over medium heat.

◆ Add the garlic and onions. Sauté until the onions are tender, 2 to 3 minutes.

◆ Add the beans, olives, oregano, and lemon pepper. Cook, stirring constantly, until the beans are crisp-tender, about 8 to 9 minutes. Add the salt toward the end of the cooking time.

◆ Transfer to a serving bowl and serve at once.

 Wine

A young Italian Chianti would be a good choice with this course.

◆ ACT IV ◆

Lemon Meringue Pie

Another Fifties favorite that never goes out of style. This extra-lemony version is a real crowd pleaser!

1 9-inch pie crust, baked and cooled	¼ cup fresh lemon juice
1 cup sugar	1 Tbsp. grated fresh lemon zest
3 Tbsp. corn starch	1 Tbsp. butter
1½ cups cold water	3 egg whites, at room temperature
3 egg yolks, lightly beaten	⅓ cup sugar

◆ Combine lemon juice and lemon zest in a small bowl. Set aside.

◆ In a medium saucepan, combine the 1 cup sugar and the corn starch. Gradually add the water and stir until smooth. Stir in the beaten egg yolks.

◆ Bring mixture to a boil over medium heat, stirring constantly. Boil for 1 minute, continuing to stir. Remove from heat. Stir in the lemon juice and zest and the butter. Allow to cool to room temperature.

◆ Preheat oven to 350°.

◆ In a medium bowl, beat egg whites with an electric mixer until foamy. Gradually beat in the ⅓ cup sugar. Continue beating until stiff peaks form.

◆ Turn cooled lemon filling into pie shell. With a rubber spatula, spread some meringue around the edges of the filling, sealing the edge of the crust. Spread remaining meringue over the rest of the surface, swirling decoratively.

◆ Bake for 15 to 20 minutes or until meringue is lightly browned. Cool completely on a wire rack.

 Grub Club Tip
For easier cutting, use a wet knife.

Coffee

As with wine, our tastes concerning coffee have evolved as gourmet coffees have become widely available and coffee-brewing methods have been perfected. It isn't necessary to subject our refined taste buds to the over-processed, over-perked brews that masqueraded as coffee in the Fifties. Serve what you normally enjoy; this is no place for nostalgia.

Curtain Call

The lemony flavor of the pie is best enhanced by a dessert wine such as a Muscat Blanc, or a California Orange Muscat—an intriguing, not-too-sweet dessert wine with a lovely pale orange color and a citrus-apricot bouquet.

NOTES

◆ ◆ ◆
Caribbean Cruise

Act I

Ginger Sesame Beef and Peppers

Paradise Punch

◆

Act II

Island Shrimp Salad

Beer or Dry White Riesling

◆

Act III

Jamaican Jerk Chicken

Cuban Black Beans and Rice

Festive Fruit Salsa

Beer or Australian Shiraz

◆

Act IV

Key Lime Mousse

Coconut Cream Liqueur

◆ CARIBBEAN CRUISE ◆

*S*ay good-bye to all your troubles as you slip away to the tropical paradise of the Caribbean islands. Feel the sun on your face while you sip a fruity rum punch and dance to the hypnotic beat of a reggae tune. Indulge your senses in a feast of flavor and a fantasy of color.

Sound inviting? It's no wonder that this chain of islands on the bright blue waters of the Caribbean Sea is a favorite vacation spot. It offers the ultimate in relaxation, native hospitality, and sensory delight. Cooking plays a major role in the island lifestyle, drawing from its rich heritage and lush landscape. The cuisine is a lively melding of Spanish, East Indian, Chinese, and British influences and showcases the exotic fruits, seafood, and spices that the islands are famous for.

So, there's no island vacation on your agenda? No problem, mon! Our Grub Club Caribbean Cruise is the next best thing. Relax, enjoy, savor the experience. You deserve it!

Decor

Be extravagant with color—the brighter the better. Vibrant cotton or paper napkins plus straw mats and plenty of baskets for serving will set the stage. If you're lucky enough to own a set of Fiestaware or other colorful pottery, there has never been a better excuse to enjoy it. The same goes for wicker or rattan furniture, trays, etc.

Display lots of fresh fruit—pineapples, coconuts, papayas, mangoes, bunches of bananas. (Guests are welcome to munch.) Mix in a few seashells, and check with your local florist, who may be able to supply you with Birds of Paradise or other tropical flowers. If your party is outdoors and extends into the evening hours, tiki torches will light the way in true island style.

Attire

Do as the natives do and dress to be cool—shorts or cotton pants (rolled up just below the knee); floppy shirts; sundresses in whites, brights, and splashy florals. Throw on a slouchy straw hat for instant shade. Ladies, turn in that stuffy leather clutch for a big straw tote, and those prim pearl earrings for a pair of generous hoops. Guys, don't bother to shave. After all, you're on vacation!

Music

Reggae music is so popular in the United States that some music stores devote entire sections to it. The choices are many but the distinctive sound is consistent. If you're feeling extravagant, or have connections, and your neighbors are tolerant, engage a steel drum band for the event.

Activities

Play traditional cruise-ship deck games, such as shuffleboard. Put out a couple of jigsaw puzzles picturing beautiful tropical scenery for the mellowest guests to enjoy. Energetic guests might appreciate a limbo contest, but better make sure there's a chiropractor on call!

◆ ACT I ◆

GINGER SESAME BEEF AND PEPPERS

Fragrant fresh ginger spices up bite-sized chunks of tender beef and crunchy peppers.

1 Tbsp. sesame seeds

¼ cup soy sauce

1 Tbsp. minced or grated fresh ginger

3 cloves garlic, minced

1 tsp. sugar

1 Tbsp. rice wine vinegar

2 green onions (including tops), thinly sliced

¼ to ½ tsp. cayenne pepper (to taste)

3 Tbsp. peanut oil

1½ lbs. boneless New York steak or tenderloin, cut into ¾ inch cubes

1 red bell pepper, seeded and cut into 1-inch squares

1 yellow bell pepper, seeded and cut into 1-inch squares

◆ Toast sesame seeds in a small frying pan over medium heat, shaking pan frequently until golden (about 3 minutes).

◆ In a medium bowl, mix sesame seeds, soy sauce, ginger, garlic, sugar, rice wine vinegar, green onions, cayenne pepper, and 1 tablespoon of the peanut oil. Add meat and stir to coat. Cover and refrigerate at least 2 hours or overnight.

◆ In a large skillet or wok, heat the other 2 tablespoons of peanut oil over medium-high heat. Add marinated meat and peppers and stir-fry until meat is cooked through (2 to 3 minutes).

◆ Serve immediately. Offer with wooden picks and have guests help themselves. Skewer a chunk of meat and pepper together and enjoy!

PARADISE PUNCH

Rum, the "national drink" of the Caribbean, blended with fruit juice and a rosy splash of grenadine is festive, flavorful, and refreshing.

2 cups orange juice

2 cups pineapple juice

¼ cup lime juice

¼ cup grenadine

1 cup dark rum

◆ Combine ingredients in a pitcher or punch bowl. Serve over ice, garnished with skewers of fresh fruit and/or little paper umbrellas.

◆ ACT II ◆

ISLAND SHRIMP SALAD

A tantalizing array of shrimp and exotic fruits, drizzled with a gingery dressing.

½ lb. medium-sized cooked shrimp

2 medium bananas, peeled and sliced

1 lemon

3 small kiwi fruit, peeled and sliced

2 small ripe avocados, peeled and cubed

1 small jicama, peeled and cut into julienne strips

1 star fruit, sliced

8 green leaf lettuce leaves

¼ cup unsweetened orange juice

3 Tbsp. mayonnaise

1 Tbsp. honey

½ tsp. ground ginger

◆ In a small bowl, whisk together orange juice, mayonnaise, honey, and ground ginger. Set aside.

◆ Squeeze one-half lemon over banana slices and toss gently to coat.

◆ Squeeze the other half of lemon over avocado chunks and toss gently.

◆ Line individual salad plates with lettuce leaves. Arrange shrimp, fruit, and jicama on each and drizzle with dressing. Serve at once.

Beverage
Beer is a good choice with Caribbean food. If you prefer to serve wine, a dry white Riesling would be appropriate here. Chilled tropical fruit juices or nectars would be good as well.

◆ ACT III ◆

JAMAICAN JERK CHICKEN

Jerk seasoning is a distinctive blend of herbs and spices unique to Jamaican cuisine, and is delicious on pork or fish as well as chicken. Its original purpose was to preserve meat, but now is enjoyed simply for its flavor. "Jerked" meat is a thriving trade in Jamaica, cooked over open fires by local street vendors.

1 to 2 fresh jalapeño peppers, seeds and membranes removed

8 cloves garlic

8 quarter-size slices (¼ inch thick) fresh ginger, peeled

½ cup (packed) parsley sprigs

¼ cup fresh basil leaves, packed, or 1 Tbsp. dried basil

2 tsp. cinnamon

1 tsp. allspice

2 tsp. salt

1 tsp. black pepper

⅓ cup yellow mustard

¼ cup lime juice

¼ cup red wine vinegar

2 Tbsp. peanut oil

2 tsp. brown sugar

8 chicken hindquarters (chicken legs with thighs attached) with skin intact

◆ In a food processor, combine the jalapeños, garlic, ginger, parsley, basil, cinnamon, allspice, salt, and black pepper. Chop finely.

◆ Add the mustard, lime juice, vinegar, peanut oil, and brown sugar. Process to a paste.

◆ Using a small spoon and fingers, work the spice mixture between the skin and meat of the chicken, and rub the remainder onto the surface. Cover and refrigerate for several hours or overnight.

◆ Bake chicken at 350° for 40 minutes. Transfer to a hot grill and cook for 10 minutes to brown.

Grub Club Tip

Instead of grilling, you may finish cooking the chicken by broiling in the oven for 4 to 5 minutes. Watch carefully.

CUBAN BLACK BEANS AND RICE

Rice and bean dishes are a staple in the Caribbean diet. This dish is sufficiently substantial and satisfying to be served as a main course, but makes a superb side dish as well.

2 15-ounce cans black beans, drained
3 Tbsp. peanut oil
3 garlic cloves, minced
1 cup chopped onions
1 tsp. ground cumin
1 tsp. ground coriander seeds
1 tsp. paprika
¼ tsp. cayenne pepper

1 cup chopped carrots
1 medium green pepper, chopped
salt and black pepper to taste
¼ cup chopped fresh parsley
1 cup tomato juice
2 medium tomatoes, chopped
6 cups cooked white rice
1 cup sour cream
¼ cup chopped green onions

◆ In a large skillet or saucepan, sauté the onions, garlic, and spices in the peanut oil until the onions are translucent.

◆ Add carrots and sauté for 3 to 4 minutes. Add green pepper and sauté for 5 minutes more.

◆ Add beans, tomato juice, tomatoes, parsley, salt, and black pepper. Simmer at least 20 minutes or until the vegetables are tender.

◆ Serve the beans on top of the hot rice. Top each serving with a dollop of sour cream and a sprinkle of chopped green onion.

Grub Club Tip
The beans may simmer as long as is necessary before serving. They just get better and better, and smell wonderful cooking.

Festive Fruit Salsa

Confetti colors and a unique, refreshing combination of flavors makes this salsa the perfect accompaniment to Jerk Chicken or other barbecued meats.

1 firm-ripe mango, peeled and diced

1 cup diced pineapple, fresh or canned

1 cup diced honeydew melon

½ cup diced red bell pepper

2 Tbsp. rice wine vinegar

Juice of ½ lime

2 Tbsp. minced cilantro

¼ cup flaked coconut

¼ to ½ tsp. crushed red pepper flakes

◆ Combine all ingredients. Refrigerate for at least 2 hours before serving.

 Grub Club Tip

If fresh mangoes are not available, substitute nectarines or cantaloupe.

Beverage

Continue with beer for this course, or serve an Australian Shiraz—a soft, full-bodied red wine with peppery overtones. (One of our favorites with spicy food).

◆ ACT IV ◆

KEY-LIME MOUSSE

Fresh fruit is the basis for many Caribbean desserts. This tart, creamy mousse is a refreshing finish to a spicy meal.

2 tsp. grated lime zest	2 Tbsp. cornstarch
¼ cup lime juice (approximately 2 limes)	pinch of salt
	⅔ cup milk
1 Tbsp. rum	1½ cups heavy cream
3 egg yolks	1 cup flaked coconut
½ cup sugar	4 bananas, sliced

◆ Spread flaked coconut in a shallow pan. Toast in a 350° oven for 10 to 15 minutes, stirring frequently until lightly golden. (Watch carefully.) Set aside. (A toaster oven works well for small toasting jobs.)

◆ Grate the zests from the limes and juice them.

◆ In a medium saucepan combine lime zest and juice with the egg yolks, sugar, cornstarch, and salt. Whisk in the milk.

◆ Cook over medium heat, stirring constantly, until custard has thickened and come to a boil, about 10 minutes.

◆ Transfer to a bowl and cool slightly. Place a sheet of plastic wrap directly on the surface to prevent a skin from forming. Place in refrigerator and chill thoroughly, about 2 hours.

◆ After the custard has chilled, whip cream in another bowl until stiff peaks form. Stir custard until smooth. Fold the whipped cream into the custard and refrigerate until serving.

◆ Just before serving, slice bananas. Place sliced bananas in the bottom of individual dessert dishes. Top with Key Lime Mousse and a sprinkling of toasted coconut.

Grub Club Tip

You may speed up the preparation time by chilling the custard in the freezer. Stir occasionally, and do not leave in for more than 30 minutes.

Coffee
Coffee may be served hot or iced. Add a splash of Coconut Cream liqueur, which has the consistency of Bailey's Irish Cream, but with a smooth coconut flavor.

Curtain Call
Try Coconut Cream liqueur over ice, or a fruit schnapps such as banana or melon. Bottles often come with recipes for exotic potions with fanciful names.

NOTES

◆ ◆ ◆
French Country Gathering

Act I

Ratatouille

———

Peppered Cheese with Apples

———

Sweet or Dry Vermouth

◆

Act II

Green Bean and Mushroom Salad

———

French Bread

———

White Burgundy

◆

Act III

Cassoulet à la Martine

———

French Bread

———

Red Burgundy

◆

Act IV

Cherry Clafouti

———

Cherry Marnier or French Sauternes

◆ FRENCH COUNTRY GATHERING ◆

*T*here is a world of difference between French "haute cuisine," which tends to be complicated and elabo-rate, and the simple, honest peasant fare that is cooked up in the country inns and home kitchens of provincial France. French country cooking relies on fresh, quality ingredients rather than fancy techniques. Dishes are enhanced with herbs, mustards, and vinegars, rather than smothered with rich sauces. The food is humble and hearty—a pleasure to prepare and a genuine joy to eat.

The different provinces of France each have their particu-lar specialties created from regional ingredients. Normandy has its apple orchards and dairies, Provence its garlic and olive oil, Bordeaux its vineyards, etc. We have taken a few liberties with our menu by combining our favorite dishes from several provinces. Despite regional diversity, there is a common passion for food and a commitment to hospitality that is shared by all French people.

If you thought French food was inaccessible, then our French Country Gathering will be a pleasant surprise. If you've always believed that the French have an incompa-rable flair for fixing fabulous food, then this meal will cer-tainly confirm it.

Decor

The setting for your French country repast should be gracious and inviting, with humble country charm. A generous kitchen table or a garden gathering spot might be considered. The table should be set informally with linens in plain colors, checks, or country florals; plus solid, serviceable dishes and glassware. Feel free to serve your wine in everyday tumblers.

Decorate without pretense, with cut flowers, such as lilacs or daisies, casually arranged in carafes or simple vases. Small terra cotta pots of herbs would be charming as well. Add some chunky candles and a rustic basket heaped with crusty French bread, and your French country table is ready to welcome your hungry guests.

Attire

Casual, comfortable, country clothing means loose cotton dresses in mellow, muted shades, and well-worn shirts and trousers. A beret (and perhaps a moustache) for the Monsieur, and a straw hat and bag for the Madame are all the accessories you'll need.

Music

The piano works of French composer Claude Debussy, or soft instrumental jazz will lend quiet elegance to your gathering.

Activities

A wine-tasting featuring French wines could be a chance to make some wonderful discoveries. Another idea is to bottle some herbal vinegars or gourmet mustards. Everyone shares in the preparation of the ingredients and the bottling, then gets to take their share home so they may continue to enjoy French flavor in their own kitchens.

◆ ACT I ◆

RATATOUILLE

A classic dish made from traditional Provençal ingredients. Ratatouille is more often served as a side dish, but cooked down a little further it becomes a delicious spread to enjoy with slices of French bread.

3 Tbsp. olive oil

1 medium yellow onion, peeled and chopped

3 to 4 garlic cloves, minced

1 medium green pepper, cored, seeded, and cut into ¼-inch dice

1 16-ounce can diced tomatoes, drained, juice reserved

1 small eggplant, peeled and cut into ½-inch cubes (about 3 cups)

1 medium zucchini, cut into ¼-inch dice

16 pitted ripe olives, halved

1 bay leaf

¾ tsp. dried thyme

½ tsp. dried basil

½ tsp. dried rosemary, crushed

½ tsp. salt

¼ tsp. freshly ground black pepper

◆ In a large saucepan, heat olive oil over medium heat. Add onion, garlic, and green pepper. Cook, stirring, until onion is translucent, 5 to 7 minutes.

◆ Stir in tomatoes. Cook 6 to 7 minutes.

◆ Add the eggplant, zucchini, olives, and all seasonings. Lower heat. Cook, covered, for 45 minutes or until vegetables are soft and mixture resembles a chunky spread. Stir occasionally. If mixture looks dry or begins to stick, add a splash or two of the reserved juice from the tomatoes.

◆ Turn mixture into a bowl. Cool. Cover and refrigerate until serving. To serve, spoon onto slices of French bread.

Grub Club Tip

If possible, make the Ratatouille the day before the event. It may be served warm, cold, or at room temperature. (We prefer it warm). It reheats easily in the microwave.

PEPPERED CHEESE WITH APPLES

Cheese and fruit are normally served as dessert after French meals. However, we feel this combination is just as welcome at the beginning of the meal.

1 4-ounce log or cake unripened goat cheese

1 tsp. mixed gourmet peppercorns (or ½ tsp. each black and white peppercorns)

½ tsp. coriander seeds

½ tsp. grated lemon zest

½ tsp. dried rosemary leaves

2 crisp apples, such as Granny Smith or Golden Delicious

Lemon juice

◆ Grind peppercorns, coriander, lemon peel, and rosemary into a coarse powder. (Use a spice mill, old coffee grinder, or a mortar and pestle.)

◆ Transfer to a sheet of wax paper. Roll cheese in pepper blend, pressing seasonings in on all sides.

◆ Core and slice apples. Sprinkle with lemon juice.

◆ Place cheese in the center of a serving plate, surround with apple slices, and garnish with sprigs of parsley or other fresh herbs. To serve, spread cheese on fruit slices.

Grub Club Tip

Serve a small bowl of tangy French Nicoise olives on the side for a flavor bonus.

Cocktail

French aperitif wines are specifically designed to awaken the taste buds and to aid digestion. These "aromatic wines" are flavored with herbs and quinine, and have a subtle, refreshing bitterness that may be described as an "acquired taste." Try sweet or dry French vermouth, or Dubonnet. Aperitif wines may be served straight, over ice, or with a splash of soda and a twist of lemon.

◆ ACT II ◆

GREEN BEAN AND MUSHROOM SALAD

The warm, rich flavors of toasted walnuts and walnut oil add distinction to this savory salad.

¾ cup coarsely chopped walnuts

1 pound fresh or frozen green beans, cut into 1½-inch pieces

1 Tbsp. walnut oil

1 Tbsp. olive oil

1 pound medium-sized fresh mushrooms, sliced

1 head Belgian endive, cut into julienne strips

1 head Bibb lettuce, torn into bite-size pieces

Dressing

2 Tbsp. red wine vinegar

1 tsp. Dijon mustard

½ tsp. dried tarragon

¼ tsp. salt

⅛ tsp. ground white pepper

¼ cup walnut oil

2 Tbsp. olive oil

◆ Preheat oven to 350°. Spread the chopped walnuts on a baking sheet and toast until light brown, 5 to 7 minutes. Cool.

◆ In a medium saucepan, bring water to a boil. Immerse the green beans and cook until crisp-tender, 5 to 7 minutes. Drain and plunge into cold water to stop the cooking. Drain well and transfer to a medium mixing bowl.

◆ In a medium skillet, heat the walnut and olive oils over medium heat. Add the mushrooms and sauté for about 3 minutes. Remove mushrooms with a slotted spoon and place in the bowl with the green beans. Cover and refrigerate until serving.

◆ To make dressing, whisk together the vinegar, mustard, tarragon, salt, and pepper. Slowly add the oils, whisking constantly until thoroughly blended. Taste and adjust seasonings.

◆ Before serving, add the toasted walnuts to the green beans and mushrooms. Pour the dressing over and toss to combine. Arrange Bibb lettuce on individual salad plates and top with green bean and mushroom mixture. Garnish with julienned endive.

BREAD

In France, bread is their staff of life—as important to their diet as rice is to Asian cuisine. It appears on the table throughout all phases of the meal, excluding dessert. Few French people bake their own bread, as even the smallest communities boast local bakeries where bread may be purchased fresh daily. The most commonly consumed French bread is the baguette, which is baked in long, thin, crusty loaves. The baguette is sliced diagonally into 1-inch slices and is served (without butter) from long, low baskets that are refilled as needed.

Seek out a bakery in your area that specializes in authentic French bread, baked daily, and purchase it the day of your event to ensure maximum freshness.

 Wine
A dry, French white Burgundy is a good choice with the salad.

◆ Act III ◆

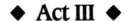

CASSOULET À LA MARTINE

A classic, hearty oven-baked stew of white beans, sausage, and meat. Grub Club member Martine Fabrizio learned much about French cooking in the time she spent in France as a student, living with a family in Avignon.

1 pound dried Great Northern beans, rinsed and picked over

2 14½-ounce cans chicken broth

1½ cups water

6 slices thick cut bacon, diced

2 pounds boneless, skinless chicken thighs, cut into 2-inch pieces

1 pound garlic sausage, or Polish kielbasa sausage, cut into ¼-inch diagonal pieces

1 large yellow onion, chopped

3 cloves garlic, minced

4 small carrots, peeled and sliced

4 ribs celery, chopped

2 14½-ounce cans diced tomatoes

1 cup dry white wine

2 bay leaves

2 tsp. dried rosemary, crushed

1 tsp. dried thyme, crushed

½ tsp. salt

Freshly ground pepper to taste

¼ cup chopped fresh parsley

1½ cups fine dry bread crumbs

½ cup finely chopped parsley (for garnish)

◆ In a large, heavy pot or Dutch oven, bring chicken broth and water to a boil. Add beans and boil for 2 minutes. Remove from heat, cover, and let soak for 1 or 2 hours.

◆ In a large skillet, cook the bacon until crisp. Remove from pan and discard all but 2 tablespoons of the drippings.

◆ Brown chicken pieces in drippings. Remove from pan with a slotted spoon. Brown sausage and remove from pan.

◆ Add onions and garlic to the pan. Cook for 2 minutes, scraping brown bits from bottom of pan. Add carrots and celery and cook 5 minutes longer. Add tomatoes (with juice), wine, bay leaves, rosemary, thyme, salt, pepper, and ¼ cup parsley. Simmer for 5 minutes.

◆ Add contents of skillet to the pot of beans. Bring to a boil. Lower heat, cover, and simmer for 30 minutes.

◆ Preheat oven to 350°.

◆ In a large, deep casserole (or 2 medium casseroles) spread a 2-inch layer of beans on the bottom. Arrange half of the sausage and all of the chicken and bacon on top of the beans. Cover with the rest of the beans and arrange the rest of the sausage on top.

◆ Slowly pour in the bean stock until it almost covers the beans. (If there isn't enough stock, add some canned chicken broth.) Spread the bread crumbs in a thick layer over the top.

◆ Bake for 1¼ hours, or until the crumbs have formed a thick, golden crust. Serve directly from the casserole, sprinkled with chopped parsley.

 ## Wine
Serve plenty of hearty French red Burgundy.

◆ ◆ ◆ ◆ ◆ ◆ ◆ ◆ ◆

◆ ACT IV ◆

CHERRY CLAFOUTI

Desserts such as this baked fruit and custard concoction are only served on special occasions in France. Cherries are the traditional choice of fruit, though peaches, apricots, and plums are good as well.

1 17-ounce can dark, sweet cherries, drained	3 eggs, lightly beaten
½ cup sifted flour	1½ cups milk
⅔ cup sugar, divided	3 Tbsp. butter, melted and cooled
Dash salt	1 pint whipping cream
	½ tsp. almond extract

◆ Preheat oven to 400°.

◆ In a large bowl, combine the flour, ½ cup of the sugar, and salt. Blend in beaten eggs. Add milk and melted butter, stirring until mixture is smooth. (Do not beat.)

◆ Butter a 9- or 10-inch quiche dish, or a 9 x 9 x 2-inch baking dish. Sprinkle in one tablespoon of the remaining sugar. Spread the cherries on the bottom of the dish. Pour in the batter.

◆ Bake for 30 minutes. Sprinkle the top with the remaining sugar. Continue baking for 15 minutes, or until the custard is firm. Let stand 5 minutes before serving.

◆ While the Clafouti is standing, whip the cream with the almond extract until soft peaks form. Serve the Clafouti in wedges, topped with a spoonful of the almond whipped cream.

Grub Club Tip
Since this dessert is best served right out of the oven, we recommend assembling and baking it at the host's house. Bring the dry ingredients pre-measured and mixed. Slip the Clafouti into the oven as the Cassoulet from Act III is coming out.

Coffee
French coffee is served strong and black, in small cups. You may prefer to serve café au lait, which is a mixture of half strong coffee and half steamed milk. (An espresso machine gives the best results.) Café au lait is a breakfast beverage in France, though we enjoy it any time.

🍷 Curtain Call

There is a grand array of delightful French brandies and liqueurs to choose from. The company that makes the popular orange-flavored Grand Marnier also makes a Cherry Marnier, which would complement the Cherry Clafouti, as would Kirsch, a cherry liqueur. French Sauternes, a dessert wine, would also be a lovely choice.

NOTES

_____

_____

_____

_____

_____

_____

_____

_____

_____

_____

_____

_____

_____

_____

_____

_____

_____

_____

_____

Greek Feast

Act I

Tzatziki with Pita Wedges

Dolmathes

Retsina

◆

Act II

Greek Salad

Pita Bread

Chardonnay

◆

Act III

Souvlakia

Oregano Baked Potatoes

Barbera D'Alba

◆

Act IV

Baklava

Ouzo

◆ Greek Feast ◆

*T*houghts of Greece inevitably conjure up visions of ancient stone ruins against a panorama of blue sky and water. Indeed, the history of Greece is as colorful as its setting. The profound impact of its past is felt in all aspects of modern Greek culture, with cooking being no exception. Some dishes still enjoyed today actually date back thousands of years. In fact, it is believed that the world's first cookbook was written in Greece around 350 B.C.

The Greeks have a particular fondness for lamb, though chicken, fish, and other meats appear on their menus as well. Lemons, olives, and oregano are hallmarks of Greek cuisine, as are feta cheese, which is made from goat's milk, and paper-thin phyllo dough, which is used in a variety of dishes from casseroles to desserts.

The Greeks are well known for their hospitality, which comes as no surprise. The food is simply too good not to share! "Kali orexi!" in the Greek language means "happy eating!," and you'll be happy to do just that.

Decor

Achieve an air of antiquity with a few simple props. Drape your dining room table with a large, solid color sheet or painter's drop cloth. (If it "puddles" on the floor, so much the better.) No fussy place settings are necessary, though generous cloth napkins will come in handy. Candles should be imposing—the widest and tallest you can find. A stately candelabra would also be effective. A platter or low basket laden with bunches of grapes creates an imposing (and edible) centerpiece.

Urns, unglazed pottery, and objects made of stone or antiqued metal make stunning accents. If you are so inclined, art supply stores and some paint stores sell "faux stone" spray paints and brush-on metal patinas that can turn the humblest flea market finds into "ancient" treasures.

Attire

It's a toga party, just like when you were in college, but with class. Think of the gods and goddesses of Greek mythology. Wrap your body in a sheet and knot it at the shoulder. Adorn your head with a garland of leaves—stores that specialize in silk flowers and greenery are a good source. Sandals are appropriate footwear, and "goddesses" may embellish their ensembles with ornate gold jewelry.

Music

Greek dance music has a distinctive sound and a lively, infectious rhythm that will bring your Greek Feast to life. The library is a rich resource for imported music.

Activities

Create your very own Greek "myth" with gods and goddesses of your own invention. The host or hostess begins telling a story, introducing the characters and a situation. He or she stops at an exciting moment and points to another guest to continue. The action proceeds until everyone has had at least one turn.

◆ ACT I ◆

TZATZKIKI

A refreshing dip made from cucumbers and yogurt.

1 medium cucumber
2 cloves garlic, minced
3 green onions, finely chopped
1 tsp. olive oil
½ tsp. white vinegar

1 tsp. finely chopped fresh dill, or
½ tsp. dried dill weed
1 cup plain, low-fat yogurt
¼ cup sour cream

◆ Peel cucumber. Cut in half lengthwise and scoop out and discard seeds.

◆ Chop cucumber and mix with garlic, green onions, olive oil, vinegar, and dill.

◆ Add yogurt and stir to combine. Fold in sour cream.

◆ Cover and chill for at least 2 hours, or overnight.

◆ Serve with wedges of pita bread and/or slices of raw zucchini.

Grub Club Tip
   Use commercial pita bread, or "borrow" the recipe for homemade pita bread from Act II.

DOLMATHES

Stuffed grape leaves are an ancient Greek "hors d'oeuvre" that is still widely enjoyed today. Grape leaves are available in jars in the specialty food section of many supermarkets.

2 cups cooked white rice

1 pound lean ground beef

3 cloves garlic, pressed

½ cup finely chopped green onions

¼ cup currants

¼ cup pine nuts or chopped almonds

½ tsp. salt

¼ tsp. black pepper

¼ cup finely chopped parsley

2 Tbsp. olive oil

1 8-ounce jar grape leaves

¼ cup lemon juice

1 10½-ounce can beef broth

1 cup water

2 lemons, cut into wedges

◆ Cook ground beef and garlic over medium-high heat until meat is brown, stirring to break up into small pieces. Drain.

◆ In a large bowl, combine meat, rice, green onions, currants, nuts, salt, pepper, parsley, and olive oil. Stir to mix.

◆ Drain grape leaves in a colander. Carefully rinse the leaves in cool running water and drain on paper towels. Cut stems off leaves with a sharp knife.

◆ Place about one tablespoon of the meat mixture on a grape leaf and roll up, tucking in ends to form a "package." Repeat until all the filling is used.

◆ In a large saucepan, arrange the rolls in layers, seam-side down. Sprinkle 1 tablespoon of lemon juice over each layer. Pour remaining lemon juice, the beef broth, and the water over the Dolmathes.

◆ Place a heavy plate or baking dish on top of the Dolmathes to hold them in place while cooking. Cover pan and cook over low heat for 1 hour.

◆ Remove from heat and allow to cool. Remove the plate and drain off all liquid. Refrigerate until serving.

◆ Serve cold or at room temperature with lemon wedges.

Grub Club Tip

Enlist the help of a partner to stuff the grape leaves. The job will go much quicker, and is actually a lot of fun.

Cocktail

Retsina is a Greek wine that is flavored with pine resin and has a distinctive pine bouquet and flavor. For most it is an acquired taste, but definitely worth trying as part of the Greek experience.

◆ ACT II ◆

GREEK SALAD

This classic salad features tangy feta cheese and Greek olives. Assemble salad just before serving.

1 head romaine lettuce

6 roma or plum tomatoes, seeded and diced, or 2 dozen cherry tomatoes, halved

2 cucumbers, peeled, seeded, and diced

8 green onions, thinly sliced

2 cups feta cheese, crumbled

About 30 black Greek olives, pitted

◆ Tear lettuce into bite-size pieces and place in a large salad bowl. Add tomatoes, cucumber, green onions, feta cheese, and olives. Pour dressing over and toss to coat.

Dressing:

¼ cup red wine vinegar

3 cloves garlic, minced

¼ tsp. salt

¼ tsp. black pepper

1 tsp. oregano, crushed

½ cup olive oil

◆ Whisk together all ingredients except olive oil. Slowly pour in oil, whisking constantly until blended.

PITA BREAD

Pita bread, or "pocket bread" is wonderfully versatile and fun to make. As with all yeast breads, it takes a little time to prepare, but the results are well worth it.

2 packages (2 Tbsp.) dry yeast	1 Tbsp. salt
½ cup warm water	3 cups whole wheat flour
1 tsp. honey	5 cups unbleached flour
2 cups warm water	cornmeal
⅓ cup olive oil	

◆ In a large mixing bowl, sprinkle yeast over the ½ cup warm water and stir in honey. Let proof for about 5 minutes, until yeast begins to foam.

◆ Stir in the 2 cups warm water, olive oil, salt, and whole wheat flour. Mix well.

◆ Stir in 4 cups of the unbleached flour, a cup at a time. Turn the dough out onto a floured board. Knead until smooth and elastic, adding more flour as necessary. Place the ball of dough in an oiled mixing bowl and turn to coat the top with oil.

◆ Cover bowl and place in a warm spot to rise—1 to 1½ hours or until dough has doubled in size.

◆ Punch the dough down and turn out onto a floured board. Let rest for 10 to 15 minutes. Cut the dough into 12 equal pieces and shape each piece into a ball. Cover with a cloth and let sit for 30 minutes.

◆ Preheat oven to 500°.

◆ With a floured rolling pin, roll each ball into an 8-inch diameter circle. Sprinkle baking sheets with cornmeal. Place circles on sheets. (Do not allow sides to touch). Cover and let rest another 30 minutes. Cover remaining rounds with a cloth.

◆ Place first baking sheet on bottom oven rack. Bake for 5 minutes. Move sheet to middle rack and place next sheet on bottom rack. Remove first sheet after 5 minutes. Continue rotation system until all circles are baked, dusting baking sheets with cornmeal before each batch.

◆ Cover pitas with a cloth immediately upon removing from oven. Though they puff up dramatically while baking, they deflate and soften as they cool. Wrap in foil or plastic wrap as soon as they are thoroughly cool.

✦ Grub Club Tip

Pitas may be reheated by wrapping in foil and placing in a 200° oven for 10 minutes.

✦ Wine

A dry white wine with firm acidity such as a Chardonnay is refreshing with the salty, tangy flavors of the salad.

◆ ACT III ◆

SOUVLAKIA

Chunks of meat are marinated for maximum tenderness, then skewered with onions and bell peppers. Lamb is the recommended meat, though beef or a combination of lamb and beef may be served.

4 pounds lamb shoulder or leg of lamb, cut into one inch cubes

2 large onions, cut into one inch chunks

2 green and 2 red bell peppers, each cut into one inch squares

2 lemons, cut into wedges

Marinade

¼ cup olive oil

Juice of one lemon

1 tsp. salt

½ tsp. pepper

1 tsp. oregano

4 cloves garlic, pressed

◆ Combine marinade ingredients in a large, flat dish. Add meat and stir to coat. Cover dish with plastic wrap and refrigerate for several hours or overnight.

◆ Thread cubes of meat, alternating with chunks of pepper and onion onto long metal skewers. Reserve remaining marinade for basting.

◆ Place skewers on a grill and cook for 10 minutes, basting. Turn and grill for 10 more minutes, basting as necessary.

◆ Remove meat and vegetables from skewers with a fork. Serve with lemon wedges.

✦ Grub Club Tip

The Souvlakia may also be broiled. Place skewers on a broiling pan and broil 6 inches from heat, 10 minutes on each side.

OREGANO BAKED POTATOES

Oregano, olive oil, and lemon juice turn ordinary potatoes into a Greek treat.

8 to 10 medium potatoes (about 4 pounds)
1 tsp. salt
⅓ cup olive oil

Juice of 1 lemon
2 tsp. oregano
1 tsp. coarse (kosher) salt

◆ Peel potatoes. Place in a large, heavy saucepan with enough water to cover potatoes completely. Add 1 teaspoon salt and bring to a boil.

◆ Boil potatoes over medium-high heat for 20 to 25 minutes, until soft but not mushy. Drain in a colander. Cool to room temperature.

◆ Preheat oven to 350°.

◆ Slice potatoes into ¼-inch-thick slices (cut large slices in half) and arrange in a 9 x 13-inch baking dish.

◆ Pour olive oil and lemon juice over potatoes. Sprinkle with oregano and coarse salt. Stir gently with a wooden spoon to combine.

◆ Bake uncovered for 30 minutes.

Wine
An Italian red wine, such as a Barbera D'Alba or a Vino Noble di Montepulciano works well with classic Greek flavors.

◆ ACT IV ◆

BAKLAVA

This sweet and flaky pastry is the most famous and popular of Greek desserts. Paper thin phyllo dough is layered with walnuts and saturated with a honey syrup. Read the recipe through carefully before you begin assembling the pastry.

Pastry
- 1 pound frozen phyllo dough, thawed
- 1 cup (½ pound) melted butter
- 3 cups finely chopped walnuts
- 1 tsp. cinnamon
- ¼ cup sugar

Honey Syrup
- ¾ cup sugar
- ¾ cup water
- ¾ cup honey
- 1 Tbsp. lemon juice

◆ In a small saucepan, combine sugar and water. Bring to a boil over medium heat. Reduce heat and simmer for 10 minutes. Remove from heat and stir in honey and lemon juice. Set aside to cool.

◆ Combine the chopped walnuts, sugar, and cinnamon.

◆ Brush a 9 x 13-inch baking pan with melted butter. Place one phyllo sheet in pan, folding to fit. Lightly brush with butter. Repeat with five more sheets, buttering each. Sprinkle the last sheet with one third of the nut mixture.

◆ Top the nut layer with four sheets of phyllo, folding to fit pan and brushing each with butter. Sprinkle with one half of remaining nut mixture.

◆ Top with four more phyllo sheets, folding to fit pan and brushing each with butter. Sprinkle with remaining nut mixture. Top with remaining sheets, brushing each with butter.

◆ Press down the top layer to compact and trim away any excess pastry from the sides with a sharp knife. Brush top with butter.

◆ With the tip of a sharp knife, score the top layer of the pastry in diagonal lines to create a diamond pattern. (Each diamond should be about 1½ x 2".)

◆ Bake in a 300° oven for 1 hour or until golden. Remove from oven and cut through the diamonds completely with a sharp knife. Pour the honey syrup over the hot pastry. Cool completely before serving.

Grub Club Tip

Phyllo dough is extremely fragile, but not too difficult to master. Follow the directions on the package carefully. As you are working, cover the unused sheets of dough with a sheet of plastic wrap or a slightly damp kitchen towel. A little vegetable oil on your fingertips helps. Work as quickly as possible.

Coffee

The Greeks drink their coffee thick, sweet, and strong. Espresso would be a reasonable facsimile. Otherwise, choose a hearty blend of regular coffee and brew a little stronger than usual. Serve with sugar.

Curtain Call

Ouzo is a clear, anise-flavored Greek liqueur. It is very potent; a little goes a long way.

NOTES

_____

_____

_____

_____

_____

_____

_____

_____

_____

_____

_____

_____

_____

_____

_____

_____

_____

_____

_____

_____

_____

_____

_____

_____

_____

New England Autumn

Act I

Clam Stuffed Pasta Shells

Marinated Mushrooms

Hot Cranberry Cider

◆

Act II

Crab and Corn Chowder

Harvest Muffins

Sauvignon Blanc

◆

Act III

Maple Glazed Roast Turkey

Wild Rice Stuffing

Creamed Butternut Squash

Zinfandel

◆

Act IV

Cranberry Walnut Pie

Calvados or Cranberry Liqueur

◆ NEW ENGLAND AUTUMN ◆

*A*utumn in the New England states is so spectacular that there are those who make annual pilgrimages to admire the lovely fall foliage. Rolling hills and winding country roads, charming old farmhouses and quaint churches all add up to a postcard prettiness that is unique to this area of the country.

New England is where "American cooking" got its start. Settlers arriving from Europe were faced with strange new foods such as shellfish, squash and pumpkins, beans and corn, and cranberries. Combining their own ingenuity with what they learned from the native Indians, they were able to create new dishes that were economical, nutritious, and flavorful. They even learned to tap into the maple trees and boil down the sap into the wonderful maple syrup that the region became famous for.

Autumn in New England is a time to appreciate the beauty and the bounty of a land that long ago gave so many people such hope, and that today gives such pleasure to its residents and visitors.

Decor

A cozy, country ambience with farmhouse flavor is what you're after. Table linens with a homespun feel, stoneware dishes, and crockery best serve the honest, substantial fare you are featuring. Consider canning jars as glassware and wooden spoons as serving utensils. Beeswax candles in simple holders or hurricane lamps provide charming warmth. Light a fire in the fireplace for an extra dose of comfort.

Raid the garden (or your local produce market) for the handsomest squashes, small pumpkins, apples, etc. to arrange in a pottery bowl or rustic basket as your centerpiece. If you grow your own herbs, a small bunch of dried herbs tied with a ribbon at each place setting will give guests something to take home and enjoy in their own kitchens.

Attire

In keeping with the "life on the farm" attitude, dress with practicality in mind. Overalls, loose fitting jeans, plaid flannel shirts, and simple cotton dresses in country prints are all appropriate. Simplicity is the key; comfort is mandatory. No high heels or "power ties" allowed.

Music

Piano music is always a pleasant option, and George Winston's "Autumn" collection on the Windham Hill label is especially appropriate here.

Activities

The brutally cold New England winters forced early settlers to turn to canning and preserving as a means of survival. Today the practice continues, but the motivation is more likely to be recreational. Organize a canning session as part of your event. It isn't as difficult as it sounds, and there are several comprehensive books on the subject that can answer all your questions. Pickles, applesauce, or a special chutney recipe are all worthy candidates for canning. The jars can be cooling as you enjoy your meal, and at the end of the evening the "fruits of your labor" can be distributed for everyone's winter pantries.

◆ ACT I ◆

CLAM STUFFED PASTA SHELLS

Giant pasta shells make convenient "packages" for creamy fillings.

8 ounces (about 2 dozen) giant shell-shaped pasta

1 Tbsp. vegetable oil

1 15-ounce container ricotta cheese

1 tsp. Worcestershire sauce

3 cloves garlic, minced

2 Tbsp. minced green onions

¼ cup chopped parsley

3 6½-ounce cans minced clams, drained

Salt and pepper to taste

Parsley sprigs for garnish

◆ In a 5- to 6-quart pan, cook pasta in 3 quarts boiling water until just tender (10 to 12 minutes). Drain. Fill pan with cold water. Add pasta and oil. When pasta has cooled, drain well and set aside.

◆ In a medium bowl, blend ricotta cheese and Worcestershire. Stir in garlic, green onions, parsley, and clams. Season to taste with salt and pepper.

◆ Fill shells with a tablespoon of filling. Press sides gently together. Arrange on a platter. If made ahead, cover and refrigerate.

◆ Before serving, garnish with sprigs of fresh parsley.

MARINATED MUSHROOMS

Herbs and spices and the tang of cider vinegar turn mushrooms into zesty hors d'oeuvres. Button mushrooms are the preferred choice, though larger mushrooms may be halved or quartered.

1 pound fresh mushrooms	Pinch of dried, crushed rosemary
1½ cups cider vinegar	2 Tbsp. olive oil
1½ cups water	¼ cup chopped fresh parsley
3 Tbsp. sugar	1 clove garlic, minced
1/4 tsp. peppercorns	½ tsp. dried basil, crushed
4 whole cloves	½ tsp. dried oregano, crushed
1-inch stick cinnamon	Salt and pepper to taste
1 bay leaf	

◆ Wash the mushrooms and pat dry. Transfer to a medium non-aluminum saucepan. Add vinegar, water, sugar, peppercorns, cloves, cinnamon, bay leaf, and rosemary.

◆ Bring the mixture to a boil. Cover the pot and let boil for 5 minutes. Remove from heat and let stand for an hour or two.

◆ Drain the mushrooms in a colander. Rinse well and pat dry with a paper towel. Remove and discard cinnamon stick, cloves, and bay leaf.

◆ Transfer mushrooms to a bowl and toss with olive oil, parsley, garlic, basil, and oregano. Season to taste with salt and pepper.

◆ Put mushrooms aside for several hours before serving. (They will keep in the refrigerator for up to 3 days.) Serve chilled or at room temperature, with toothpicks.

HOT CRANBERRY CIDER

A bracing beverage for blustery weather.

2 quarts apple cider	1 tsp. whole cloves
1 quart cranberry juice	1 lemon, thinly sliced
¼ cup brown sugar (packed)	1 cup rum
4 whole cinnamon sticks	

◆ Combine all ingredients in a large saucepan or kettle. Heat to boiling. Reduce heat and simmer 15 to 20 minutes. Serve in mugs.

◆ ACT II ◆

CRAB AND CORN CHOWDER

The subtle sweetness of crab and corn in a delicate, creamy broth, accented with a hint of nutmeg.

1 medium onion, chopped

2 cloves garlic, minced

1 medium all-purpose potato, peeled and cut into ½-inch cubes

1 rib celery, coarsely chopped

2 medium carrots, coarsely chopped

4 Tbsp. butter

3 Tbsp. flour

2 cups chicken broth (may used canned)

½ tsp. salt

¼ tsp. ground white pepper

¼ tsp. nutmeg

2 cups milk

8 ounces crabmeat, fresh or canned; or surimi, shredded

1 12-ounce can whole kernel corn, drained

◆ In a large saucepan, melt the butter over medium heat. Add the onion and garlic and cook until the onion is translucent.

◆ Stir in the flour and cook until flour is absorbed, about one minute.

◆ Slowly pour in the chicken broth, stirring constantly. Bring mixture to a boil. Add potato, carrots, celery, salt, pepper, and nutmeg. Reduce heat to medium-low. Cover and simmer until potato is tender, about 20 minutes.

◆ Increase heat to medium-high. Add milk, crabmeat, and corn. Taste and adjust seasonings. Cook until heated through, about 5 minutes.

◆ Serve immediately. Or, chowder may be made ahead and slowly reheated.

HARVEST MUFFINS

Perfect for your autumn bread basket.

1 cup all-purpose flour	¼ tsp. cinnamon
½ cup whole wheat flour	½ cup milk
½ cup sugar	½ cup canned pumpkin
2 tsp. baking powder	¼ cup butter, melted
½ tsp. salt	1 egg, lightly beaten

◆ Preheat oven to 400° Grease the bottoms of 12 muffin cups.

◆ In a medium mixing bowl, combine the dry ingredients. Add milk, pumpkin, melted butter, and egg. Mix just until combined. (Do not overmix—batter should be lumpy.)

◆ Fill muffin cups ⅔ full. Bake 18 to 20 minutes. Remove from pan immediately.

Wine

The subtle sweetness of the Crab and Corn Chowder will be enhanced by a Sauvignon Blanc.

◆ ACT III ◆

MAPLE GLAZED ROAST TURKEY
with WILD RICE STUFFING

Don't expect leftovers when you serve this succulent roast turkey, glazed with Vermont maple syrup and stuffed with a savory blend of sausage and wild rice.

12-pound turkey	1 Tbsp. soy sauce
2 tsp. salt	2 cups dark rum
1 tsp. pepper	2 Tbsp. flour
½ cup pure maple syrup	

Stuffing

2⅔ cup chicken broth

1 cup uncooked brown rice

⅓ cup uncooked wild rice

1 Tbsp. vegetable oil

1 large onion, chopped

3 cloves garlic, minced

¼ cup celery, chopped

½ pound country sausage, casings removed

¼ pound mushrooms, chopped

1 tsp. dried sage

1 tsp. dried thyme

¼ tsp. pepper

¼ cup chopped walnuts

◆ In a medium saucepan, bring chicken broth, brown rice, and wild rice to a boil over medium-high heat. Reduce heat to low; cover and simmer about 45 minutes or until all liquid is absorbed. Uncover and set aside.

◆ In a large skillet, sauté the onion, garlic, and celery in the vegetable oil over medium-high heat until the onion begins to brown, about 5 minutes.

◆ Add sausage to the skillet and cook until no longer pink, about 6 minutes.

◆ Add mushrooms, sage, thyme, and pepper. Cook for 3 to 5 minutes. Stir in cooked rice and chopped walnuts. Set aside to cool slightly.

◆ Preheat oven to 350°.

◆ Remove giblets from turkey cavity and wash the turkey inside and out under cold running water. Pat dry with paper towels.

◆ Stuff turkey, including neck cavity, with stuffing. (Any remaining stuffing may be baked separately in a covered baking dish for about 40 minutes).

◆ Rub the turkey with salt and pepper and place breast-side up in a roasting pan.

◆ In a small bowl, combine maple syrup and soy sauce. Brush mixture onto turkey with a basting brush. Insert a meat thermometer into the breast of the turkey, making sure that it does not contact bone. Pour rum into roasting pan and place in oven.

◆ Cook until temperature on meat thermometer registers 170°. Allow 3 to 4 hours for cooking. Check package for roasting times, taking into account that a stuffed turkey takes approximately an hour longer to cook than an unstuffed turkey. Baste with pan juices, using a turkey baster, every 15 to 20 minutes. Tent with foil if it appears to be browning too quickly.

◆ Remove from oven and allow to sit for at least 15 minutes before carving.

◆ Skim the fat from the pan juices and reserve 1 tablespoon of fat. In a small saucepan, combine ¼ cup of the pan juices with the flour and 1 tablespoon of fat. Stir over medium heat until smooth. Blend in the rest of the pan juices and stir with a wire whisk until gravy has thickened.

CREAMED BUTTERNUT SQUASH

A perfect accompaniment to roast turkey and a delightful alternative to mashed potatoes or yams.

4 pounds butternut squash, peeled, seeded, and cut into 2-inch chunks

4 Tbsp. butter, cut into small pieces

2 Tbsp. pure maple syrup

½ tsp. ground nutmeg

1 tsp. salt, or to taste

◆ Pour water into the lower part of a steamer to within one inch of the top pan. Bring to a boil.

◆ Place squash into top pan and cover. Steam for about 30 minutes, or until soft.

◆ Transfer squash to a heavy skillet and mash with a potato masher until smooth. (If your skillet has a nonstick coating that could be damaged, transfer squash to a bowl for mashing and then to the skillet).

◆ Cook mashed squash over medium heat, stirring almost constantly, until purée is dry. Stir in the butter, maple syrup, nutmeg, and salt.

◆ Serve at once, sprinkled with a little more nutmeg.

Wine
The savory sausage stuffing in the roast turkey demands a full-bodied red wine, such as a California Zinfandel.

◆ ACT IV ◆

CRANBERRY WALNUT PIE

Tangy cranberries and crunchy walnuts baked into a lovely lattice-top pie. We've included a "from scratch" pie crust recipe, but feel free to use a packaged mix or frozen crust if time is short. Makes one 9-inch pie.

Crust

2½ cups unbleached flour

1 tsp. salt

6 Tbsp. unsalted butter, room temperature

½ cup shortening

5 to 6 Tbsp. ice water

1 egg yolk beaten with 1 Tbsp. milk

Filling

3½ cups firm, unblemished
cranberries

1 cup coarsely chopped walnuts

1 cup sugar

4 Tbsp. flour

¾ cup raisins

¼ cup orange juice

1 tsp. grated orange zest

3 Tbsp. butter, melted

1 tsp. cinnamon

⅛ tsp. salt

◆ For the crust, combine the flour and salt in a large mixing bowl. Add the butter and rub it into the flour with your fingers until it disappears. Cut in the shortening with a pastry blender until it forms pieces the size of peas.

◆ Sprinkle the mixture with 1 tablespoon ice water and mix with a fork for about 20 seconds. Continue adding ice water a tablespoon and then a tea-spoon or a few drops at a time, mixing until the dough forms a ball. Divide dough in half. Wrap each half in plastic wrap and chill for an hour.

◆ Place half of the well-chilled dough on a floured surface. (Leave the other half in the refrigerator). Roll out to a circle about 5 inches larger than the diameter of the pie pan. Fold it in half and center it in the pan, then gently unfold and ease to fit. Chill for an hour.

◆ While bottom crust is chilling, prepare filling. Wash the cranberries under cold running water and pat dry with paper towels. Chop coarsely (you may use a food processor). Combine cranberries with rest of filling ingredients and mix well.

◆ Preheat oven to 400°. Spread filling into chilled pie shell.

◆ Roll out second half of pastry dough and cut into ½- inch wide strips. Using a pastry brush, coat each strip with the egg and milk mixture. Lay half of the strips across pie in one direction; weave remaining strips through in opposite direction to form a lattice. Pinch edges together and trim off any excess dough.

◆ Bake for about 1 hour until crust is golden brown. If edge begins to brown too quickly, cover with a loose strip of foil.

◆ Cool before serving. Serve with a scoop of vanilla ice cream and garnish, if you wish, with small, brightly colored autumn leaves.

☕ Coffee

Cups of rich, robust coffee may be served with a splash of brandy. Alternatively, commemorate the Boston Tea Party with a steaming pot of tea. A cinnamon-spice blend would be a good choice.

🍷 Curtain Call

The tang of fresh cranberries is deliciously captured in Bogg's Cranberry Liqueur. Calvados, an apple brandy, is another option.

NOTES

_____

_____

_____

_____

_____

_____

_____

_____

_____

_____

_____

_____

_____

_____

_____

_____

_____

NOTES

◆ ◆ ◆
East Indian Escapade

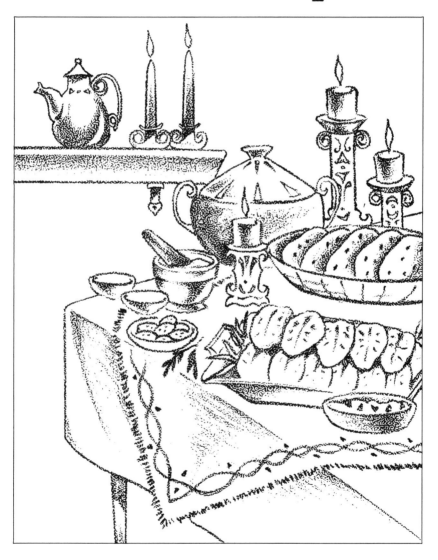

Act I

Samosas

Spiced Cucumber Wedges

Beer or Riesling

◆

Act II

Mulligatawny

Chappati

Beer or Riesling

◆

Act III

Indian Sunburst Chicken

Basmati Rice with Peas

Cucumber Raita

Apricot Chutney

Beer or Australian Shiraz

◆

Act IV

Indian Rice Pudding

Ginger Liqueur or Ginger Brandy

◆ East Indian Escapade ◆

*W*hen we think of Indian food we tend to think first of curries, and though curries do play an important role, they are only part of a much larger picture. The cuisine of India is as complex and diverse as its culture. Much of India's diet is influenced by the beliefs of its various religious groups. Some groups are strict vegetarians. Other groups eat meat with the exception of beef, as they consider cows sacred. Still other groups have few, if any restrictions. All Indian cooking features the creative use of spices, grains, and legumes, and the meals are as visual as they are flavorful.

A typical Indian meal is accompanied by an assortment of condiments that add contrast and dietary balance to the menu. These condiments include fruit or vegetable chutneys, which are spicy relishes, and raitas, which are yogurt-based dishes designed to cool and refresh the palate. In addition, most Indian meals include some kind of unleavened bread. These elements, along with substantial main and side dishes, add up to meals that are healthful, economical, and lots of fun to eat.

Our "East Indian Escapade" is a culinary journey to a land where cooking is an adventure, and dining an experience. This is one journey you won't want to miss.

Decor

Exotic elegance sets the stage for your escapade. Drape your table in bazaar-bright, hand-dyed fabrics, and use plenty of gold and brass accents. Large import stores stock a wealth of affordable items, including brass candlesticks and trivets, carved boxes, and other Indian treasures. Metallic gold spray paint is an easy way to add a touch of gilt to found objects.

Especially easy on the budget are gold paper doilies, which bear a striking resemblance to the gold filigree and carvings found on many Indian decorative objects. Use as is, snip them apart and use the strips as napkin rings, or wrap pieces around votive candle holders. The effect is stunning.

Lighting should be low and mysterious, best accomplished with candles of varying heights. Burning incense will add yet another sensual element to the experience. The alluring fragrance of incense is compatible with the aromatic spices used in Indian cooking.

Attire

The climate of India is hot, which calls for loose, comfortable cottons or silks. Many of the women still wear saris, which are long pieces of fabric draped like dresses. Bold gold or brass jewelry, especially bracelets, add exotic glamour. Men may fashion turbans from scarves or strips of material.

Music

Indian sitar music has a haunting and distinctive sound that will transport you instantly to the land of silks and spices. Works by the famed sitarist Ravi Shankar are widely available.

Activities

Seek out commercial games with Indian origins, such as Parcheesi. Another game that is fun for groups of all sizes is Jenga, in which players take turns removing blocks from a wooden tower, while trying to retain the structure's stability. The first person to topple the tower loses. It's a game you'll want to play at all your parties!

◆ ACT I ◆

SAMOSAS

These deep-fried, stuffed pastries make perfect party food.

Filling

2 cups peeled and diced potatoes

2 Tbsp. vegetable oil

½ tsp. cumin seeds

1 medium onion, chopped

1-inch piece fresh ginger, peeled and chopped

1 tsp. coriander powder

½ tsp. turmeric

½ tsp. cayenne pepper

1 tsp. salt

½ tsp. anise seed

¾ cup frozen green peas, thawed

Juice of 1 lemon

Pastry

2½ cups flour

½ tsp. salt

½ tsp. baking powder

3 Tbsp. vegetable oil

½ cup water

2 cups vegetable oil (for deep-frying)

◆ Boil the diced potatoes until tender, about 20 minutes. Drain and set aside.

◆ In a heavy skillet, heat the 2 tablespoons vegetable oil over medium heat. Add the cumin seeds and stir until the seeds are brown. Add the onion and ginger and stir until coated with oil. Add the coriander, turmeric, cayenne, salt, and anise seed plus a dash of water. Cook until the mixture is well browned. Remove from heat. Stir in potatoes, peas, and lemon juice. Set aside to cool.

◆ For the pastry, sift the flour, salt, and baking powder into a large bowl. Pour in the oil. Knead mixture, gradually adding water, until a stiff dough is formed.

◆ Divide the dough into 16 equal parts and roll them into balls. With a rolling pin, roll each ball into a thin circle, about 4-inches in diameter. Cut circles in half. Form a cone by folding a half-circle in half and pressing cut edges together with moistened fingers. Crimp tightly. Fill cone with potato and pea mixture. Seal the open end of the cone with moistened fingers, crimping tightly. Prepare all the Samosas and cover with a damp dishcloth.

◆ Heat oil in a frying pan over medium heat. Fry Samosas, 4 or 5 at a time for 2 to 3 minutes until golden brown on all sides. Drain on paper towels. Serve warm or at room temperature.

Spiced Cucumber Wedges

This cool, crunchy snack would be just as welcome at a summer barbecue.

3 small cucumbers

1 lemon

½ tsp. cumin seeds

½ tsp. salt

⅛ tsp. cayenne pepper

⅛ tsp. freshly ground black pepper

◆ In a small frying pan, stir the cumin seeds over medium heat until they darken slightly and smell toasted and aromatic. Grind to a powder in a spice grinder or a mortar and pestle. Combine with salt, cayenne pepper, and black pepper.

◆ Peel cucumbers and cut in half crosswise. Cut each half into 4 sections lengthwise. Chill.

◆ Just before serving, arrange cucumber wedges on a plate. Sprinkle with fresh lemon juice, then with the spice mixture. Serve at once.

Cocktail

Though alcoholic beverages are not a major part of Indian culture, beer goes quite well with Indian food. Choose an Indian beer if you can find one, or a flavorful English beer or ale. If you prefer to serve wine, a dry white Riesling would be a good choice.

◆ ACT II ◆

MULLIGATAWNY

There are many versions of this popular curry-flavored soup, all slightly different. The name translates as "pepper water," and though it is spicy, as its name implies, it is quite substantial and not at all "watery."

2 medium onions, chopped

3 cloves garlic, minced

2 Tbsp. peanut oil

2 14-ounce cans chicken broth

3 medium carrots, chopped

2 medium apples, peeled and chopped

½ cup flaked coconut

1 to 2 Tbsp. curry powder (to taste)

1 Tbsp. lemon juice

3 whole cloves

1 bay leaf

2 tsp. salt

1 cup milk

¼ cup flour

◆ In a large saucepan or Dutch oven, heat the peanut oil over medium heat. Add the onions and garlic and cook until the onions are translucent.

◆ Add the chicken broth, carrots, apples, coconut, curry powder, lemon juice, cloves, bay leaf, and salt. Bring to a boil. Reduce heat, cover, and simmer for 1 hour.

◆ Transfer half of the soup to a blender. Purée and return to pan.

◆ Stir together milk and flour. Add to soup. Cook and stir until slightly thickened. Soup may be made ahead and gently reheated.

Grub Club Tip

The flavor and degree of hotness of commercial curry powders varies. If your curry is mild, and you like your soup spicy, add a pinch or two of cayenne pepper.

CHAPPATI

This bread is just one of several types that are commonly served at Indian meals. The chappati resemble tortillas in appearance, but have a nutty, whole-wheat flavor.

2 cups whole-wheat flour
½ cup all-purpose flour
1 tsp. salt

¼ cup melted butter
¾ cup warm water

◆ In a large mixing bowl, combine the flours and salt. Sprinkle melted butter and half a cup of the water over the mixture and stir with a fork.

◆ Knead dough, adding enough additional water, a tablespoon at a time, until the dough is firm and supple. Knead for about 10 more minutes. Cover with a damp cloth and let the dough rest for 30 minutes.

◆ Separate the dough into 8 pieces, and form each piece into a round. Flatten one of the rounds with the palm of your hand. On a floured surface, roll the round into a paper-thin circle about 8-inches in diameter, turning several times so that both sides are well floured. Repeat with the remaining pieces of dough.

◆ Heat a heavy skillet (preferably cast iron) over medium heat. Fry the chappati one at a time about 1½ to 2 minutes on each side, turning when the bottom is flecked with brown.

◆ Stack fried chappati in a napkin-lined dish, covered to keep warm.

 ### Grub Club Tip
Chappati may be wrapped in foil and gently reheated in a 200° oven.

Beverage
Beer or ale is a good accompaniment to the curry flavors of the soup. If you prefer to serve wine, a cool, refreshing white Riesling would be a good choice.

◆ ACT III ◆

INDIAN SUNBURST CHICKEN

Classic Indian spices give this baked chicken dish a glorious golden-red color.

2 tsp. ground cumin

4 tsp. paprika

½ tsp. cayenne pepper

1 Tbsp. ground turmeric

½ tsp. ground ginger

1 tsp. freshly ground pepper

1 tsp. salt

3 cloves garlic, mashed to a pulp

6 Tbsp. lemon juice

4 pounds boneless, skinless chicken pieces (breasts, thighs, or a combination)

3 Tbsp. vegetable oil

◆ In a small bowl, combine the spices, garlic, and lemon juice, mixing into a paste.

◆ Rub or brush the paste over all surfaces of the chicken pieces. Arrange the chicken in a shallow baking dish. Cover and refrigerate for at least 3 hours.

◆ Preheat the oven to 350°. Brush the tops of the chicken pieces with the vegetable oil.

◆ Bake the chicken for 20 minutes. Turn the pieces over and bake for another 25 minutes, or until chicken is tender. Baste occasionally with pan juices.

◆ Arrange on a platter and serve hot.

BASMATI RICE WITH PEAS

Versions of this popular and versatile side-dish show up at many Indian meals. Basmati rice is a particularly fragrant variety of long-grain rice.

2 cups Basmati rice

3 Tbsp. vegetable oil

1 tsp. whole cumin seeds

1 medium onion, peeled and chopped

2 cups fresh peas, or frozen peas, thawed

1 tsp. salt

2⅔ cups water

◆ Rinse the rice to remove starchy residue and drain. Soak the rice for 30 minutes in water to cover and drain well.

◆ In a heavy pot, heat the oil over medium heat. Add the cumin seeds and stir for a few seconds.

◆ Add the chopped onion and fry until the onion begins to brown. Add the rice, salt, and peas. Sauté for 3 to 4 minutes until all ingredients are well coated with oil.

◆ Add the water and bring to a boil. Cover the pan and turn the heat to the lowest setting possible. Cook for 25 minutes.

◆ Remove the pot from the heat and allow to sit for 5 minutes. Fluff gently with a fork before serving.

Grub Club Tip

For best results, use a pot with a very tight-fitting lid. Never lift the lid while the rice is cooking.

Cucumber Raita

A cool, creamy contrast to spicy dishes. Serve as a condiment alongside the chicken and rice.

2 cups plain yogurt

1 small cucumber

2 Tbsp. finely chopped fresh mint

½ tsp. cumin seeds

¼ tsp. salt

Freshly ground pepper to taste

◆ Peel and grate the cucumber. Drain in a sieve and press gently to release excess moisture.

◆ Place cumin seeds in a small, heavy frying pan. Stir the seeds over medium heat until they darken slightly and smell toasted and aromatic. Grind to a powder in a spice grinder or mortar and pestle.

◆ Spoon yogurt into a medium bowl. Beat lightly with a fork or whisk until smooth and creamy.

◆ Blend in the grated cucumber, mint, cumin, salt, and pepper. Cover and refrigerate until ready to serve.

 Grub Club Tip

The Raita may be made the day before the event.

APRICOT CHUTNEY

Serve this spicy, fruity relish the same way you would serve cranberry sauce with turkey, or applesauce with pork chops.

½ pound dried apricots, cut into pieces

2 cups hot water

1 Tbsp. chopped fresh ginger

5 cloves garlic, chopped

⅔ cup red wine vinegar

1 cup sugar

⅛ tsp. salt

⅛ tsp. cayenne pepper

½ cup golden raisins

¼ cup currants

◆ Put the apricot pieces in a bowl. Pour in the 2 cups of hot water and let soak for 1 hour.

◆ In a blender or food processor, blend the ginger and garlic with 2 table-spoons of the vinegar until smooth.

◆ Transfer the apricots and their soaking liquid to a heavy, non-aluminum pot. Stir in the garlic-ginger mixture, plus the remaining vinegar, sugar, salt, and cayenne.

◆ Bring to a boil. Lower heat and simmer, stirring frequently, for 45 minutes. Be careful that the chutney doesn't stick.

◆ Add the raisins and currants. Cook, stirring frequently for 30 minutes, or until the chutney thickens and appears glazed. (It will thicken slightly more as it cools).

◆ Cool and store covered in the refrigerator.

Grub Club Tip

Make the chutney a day or two before the event, to give the flavors a chance to blend and mellow.

Wine

Continue to serve beer or ale with this course, or perhaps try a soft, full-bodied Australian Shiraz, or a Beaujolais-Villages.

◆ ACT IV ◆

INDIAN RICE PUDDING

This rice pudding, called firni, uses rice flour rather than whole grain rice for a smooth, creamy consistency. Rose water and cardamom add exotic flavor and aroma. Grub Club member Jonathan Shields sampled this dish in an Indian restaurant in New York several years ago, and made it his mission to recreate what he believes is "the holy grail of desserts."

4 cups (1 quart) whole milk	1 Tbsp. rose water
1/2 cup rice flour	1/2 cup slivered almonds
1 cup sugar	Cardamom powder
3 Tbsp. currants or raisins	

◆ In a heavy saucepan, bring milk to a boil over medium-high heat.

◆ Gradually sift in rice flour, whisking constantly with a wire whisk until thoroughly blended and smooth. Lower heat to medium. Continue cooking for 8 minutes, stirring constantly with a wooden spoon.

◆ Add sugar and cook for 5 to 7 minutes, stirring constantly just until mixture thickens. (Be careful not to overcook, or pudding may become "gummy".)

◆ Remove from heat. Stir in currants and rose water. Pour into a serving bowl and let sit until slightly cooled. Cover and refrigerate until serving.

◆ Serve well-chilled, in small bowls, sprinkled with ground cardamom and slivered almonds.

Grub Club Tip

If you wish, you may decorate your dessert with shapes cut from tissue-thin sheets of edible silver, called *vark*, which is available at some Indian markets.

☕ Coffee

Both coffee and tea are popular Indian beverages. We sprinkled a dash of cardamom powder over our ground coffee before brewing, for a touch of exotic flavor. A Darjeeling tea, perhaps flavored with cinnamon or orange, would be delicious as well.

🍷 Curtain Call

Though there are no liqueurs that are indigenous to India, the spiciness of a ginger liqueur or a ginger brandy would finish off the meal nicely. If you can find Crème de Roses, a liqueur flavored with rose essence, try it with the dessert.

NOTES

_____

_____

_____

_____

_____

_____

_____

_____

_____

_____

_____

_____

_____

_____

_____

Notes

A Christmas Carol

Act I

Cheddar Brandy Spread

Cucumber Tea Sandwiches

Wassail

◆

Act II

Christmas Salad

Cranberry Tea Bread

Rosé Cabernet or Dry Riesling

◆

Act III

Standing Rib Roast

Oven Roasted Vegetables

Yorkshire Pudding

Merlot or Cabernet-Merlot

◆

Act IV

Sherried Fruit Trifle

Cream Sherry

◆ A Christmas Carol ◆

*M*any of the customs and images that we associate
with Christmas originated in England in the mid-
1800's. Literature from this period, including the works of
Charles Dickens, helped to define and establish the holiday
traditions that have followed us into the present. Lavish
feasts, Christmas trees and Christmas cards, caroling, and
decorating our homes with greenery are as much a part of
our Yuletide festivities today as they were during the time
when the beloved story "A Christmas Carol" was written.

As the Grub Club celebrates Christmas, we return to our
roots, so to speak, with a menu that is classically English.
Steaming Wassail, hearty roast beef and Yorkshire pudding,
and a tempting Trifle are featured in a feast that promises to
evoke the holiday spirit in even the Scrooges among us.

These days, with life's hectic pace and the over-commer-
cialization of the holiday season, it's hard to imagine the
"comfort and joy" of Christmases past. Our Grub Club
"Christmas Carol" is a nostalgic visit to a time and place
where Christmas was a chance to reflect and rejoice, and to
share abundant good cheer with family and friends.

Decor

Most of us decorate our homes in some manner for the holidays, and collect cherished mementos that we look forward to displaying year after year. Old-fashioned, traditional decorations and plenty of greenery will create just the right look for your Christmas gathering.

Holly, ivy, and mistletoe were used generously in English homes of this era, and are still popular and readily available today. Evergreen wreaths and garlands are a welcome touch anywhere. A centerpiece for your table need be no more than a few well-placed candles and some fresh boughs or sprigs of greenery. Christmas trees may be any size desired. If space is at a premium, consider a small tabletop tree that fits neatly into a corner. Trees may be simply adorned with strings of cranberries and popcorn, or lavishly decked out with heirloom treasures. Either approach is appropriate.

Other accessories might include old-fashioned teddy bears, antique dolls and toys, an old wagon or sled, and a classic nutcracker. Rooms should glow with candlelight (white candles for authenticity) and firelight if you have a fireplace.

Attire

Seek out holiday finery with old-fashioned flavor in luxurious fabrics such as satin, brocade, or velvet. Gentlemen will look "gentlemanly" in ties and vests. Proper ladies' attire might include a long-sleeved, high-neck blouse and a sweeping skirt. Of course, wear whatever makes you feel most festive.

Music

Though more and more contemporary recording artists are producing their version of Christmas music, the best musical selections for your event are traditional Christmas carols sung by choirs. A fine example is the Mormon Tabernacle Choir, whose rich, jubilant renditions of traditional carols capture the Christmas essence to perfection. The score to Tchaikovsky's "The Nutcracker" would be another good choice.

ACTIVITIES

There are a host of holiday activities that your group may indulge in. A gift exchange of kitchen related items, for instance, is fun for all. Each person brings an inexpensive wrapped gift, which is assigned a number upon arrival. Later in the evening, guests draw numbers from a hat and open the corresponding gift.

Hosts may invite their guests to help trim the tree, or go caroling. The group could attend a performance of "The Nutcracker" before or after the meal. And if you're having a white Christmas, build a "snow chef" in the front yard, complete with apron and kitchen implements.

◆ ACT I ◆

CHEDDAR BRANDY SPREAD

A rich, mellow blend of cheese, fruit, and nuts, accented with brandy.

8 ounces cheddar cheese, grated	¼ cup chopped pecans
3 Tbsp. butter, softened	¼ cup currants
2 Tbsp. cognac or other brandy	

◆ In a bowl, mix cheese, butter and brandy until thoroughly blended and smooth. Stir in pecans and currants.

◆ Refrigerate at least 1 hour before serving. Serve with crackers, or slices of apple or pear.

Grub Club Tip
A food processor may be used to grate the cheese and to blend in the butter and brandy.

Cucumber Tea Sandwiches

These festive little sandwiches might ordinarily be served at an afternoon tea, but for our purposes they make charming hors d'oeuvres.

1 loaf thinly sliced, firm white bread

2 medium cucumbers

1 8-ounce package cream cheese, softened

3 Tbsp. Stilton cheese, crumbled

1 Tbsp. minced green onion

2 Tbsp. minced parsley

½ tsp. dill

1 small jar pimento strips

1 small bunch watercress (optional)

◆ Cut bread slices into about 32 rounds or Christmas shapes with cookie cutters.

◆ With a vegetable peeler, trim lengthwise strips of peel from cucumbers to create a striped effect. Cut cucumbers into thin slices. Blot with paper towels.

◆ In a small bowl, combine cream cheese, Stilton, green onion, parsley, and dill.

◆ Spread bread shapes with cheese mixture. Top each with a slice of cucumber. Garnish with optional watercress and a strip or two of pimento.

Grub Club Tip

Assemble sandwiches as close as possible to serving time to avoid sogginess.

WASSAIL

A traditional symbol of Christmas merriment. This heartwarming wine punch is potent—a small serving packs a lot of cheer!

3 small cooking apples

½ cup brandy

¼ cup brown sugar, packed

¾ cup water

2 cinnamon sticks, broken into one inch pieces

6 whole cloves

6 whole allspice

1 bottle dry red wine (preferably claret or Bordeaux)

1½ cups dry sherry

◆ Core apples and peel a strip from the top of each. Place apples in a small baking dish or casserole.

◆ Combine brandy and brown sugar in a small saucepan. Bring just to boiling. Pour over apples and cover dish with foil. Bake in a 350° oven for 35 to 40 minutes or until tender.

◆ Drain apples, reserving syrup. Combine syrup and water in a large saucepan or Dutch oven. Add spices.

◆ Bring to boiling. Reduce heat and cover. Simmer for 10 minutes. Stir in wine and sherry and heat through.

◆ Transfer to a punch bowl and float baked apples on top. Or, serve right from the pan.

◆ ACT II ◆

CHRISTMAS SALAD

A guest at our Christmas Grub Club dinner proclaimed, "This is the kind of salad that makes me wonder why I don't eat salads more often!"

1 small head romaine lettuce, torn into bite-size pieces

1 small head Boston lettuce, torn into bite-size pieces

1 bunch green onions, thinly sliced (including tops)

1 large apple, coarsely chopped

½ lemon

4 tangerines, peeled and separated into sections

¾ cup chopped walnuts

Cranberry Vinaigrette
6 Tbsp. cranberry juice

¼ cup cider vinegar

2 tsp. Dijon mustard

2 tsp. vegetable oil

1 Tbsp. honey

½ tsp. ground ginger

◆ Combine dressing ingredients in a jar with a tightly fitting lid. Shake vigorously. Refrigerate for at least 1 hour.

◆ Preheat oven to 350°. Spread chopped walnuts on a cookie sheet and toast for about 15 minutes, stirring occasionally. (Watch carefully.) Cool and set aside.

◆ Make a small slit near the seam of each tangerine section and remove seeds. Squeeze lemon juice over chopped apple and toss to coat.

◆ Just before serving, toss salad greens, green onions, chopped apple, and tangerine sections with Cranberry Vinaigrette. Arrange on individual salad plates. Sprinkle each serving with toasted walnuts.

CRANBERRY TEA BREAD

A perfect holiday bread to enjoy all season long. Especially delightful with the Christmas Salad.

2½ cups flour	1 cup milk
1 cup sugar	¼ cup orange juice
3½ tsp. baking powder	1 egg
1 tsp. salt	1 cup cranberries, chopped
3 Tbsp. vegetable oil	½ cup chopped walnuts

◆ Preheat oven to 350°. Grease and flour a 9 x 5 x 3-inch loaf pan.

◆ In a large mixing bowl, combine flour, sugar, baking powder, and salt. Add vegetable oil, milk, orange juice, and egg. Stir to moisten.

◆ With an electric mixer, beat on medium speed for about 30 seconds, scraping down sides of bowl. Fold in cranberries and walnuts.

◆ Pour into prepared pan. Bake for 55 to 65 minutes, or until a wooden pick inserted into the center comes out clean.

◆ Remove from pan. Let cool completely (preferably several hours or overnight) before slicing. Cut into thin slices. Cut each slice in half and arrange in a circle on a serving plate.

 Wine

Enjoy a dry Rosé Cabernet or a dry Riesling with this course.

◆ ACT III ◆

STANDING RIB ROAST

This classic English main dish is an event in itself! The pan juices impart their rich flavor to the accompanying vegetables and Yorkshire Pudding.

1 standing rib roast (about 7 pounds)
2 to 3 tsp. coarse (kosher) salt
freshly ground pepper to taste
¼ cup flour

1 cup beef broth
1 cup water
2 Tbsp. butter, room temperature
Salt and pepper to taste

◆ Preheat oven to 425°.

◆ Place roast in roasting pan. (If you do not own a roasting pan, inexpensive disposable foil pans work nicely). Sprinkle roast with coarse salt and pepper. Insert a meat thermometer into the thickest part of the roast, making sure that the tip does not touch bone.

◆ Cook roast for 30 minutes. Lower heat to 325° and cook until the meat thermometer registers 120° for rare or 130° for medium. (About 15 minutes per pound).

◆ Remove roast from oven and transfer to a serving platter. Cover loosely with foil and allow to stand for 15 minutes before carving.

◆ While the roast is standing, prepare the gravy. Pour ¼ cup of the drippings from the roasting pan into a small saucepan. Over high heat, gradually add flour and whisk until smooth. Slowly pour in broth and water, whisking constantly. Cook until thickened, about 5 minutes.

◆ Remove gravy from heat and stir in butter. Season with salt and pepper to taste.

Oven-Roasted Vegetables

Hearty vegetables are lightly steamed, then drizzled with pan juices and roasted to perfection.

12 small new potatoes, scrubbed and halved

3 slender carrots, pared and cut into 2-inch lengths

3 medium turnips, pared and cut into 6 or 8 wedges

2 to 3 parsnips or 1 rutabaga, cut into 2-inch chunks

2 to 3 Tbsp. beef drippings from roast

Coarse (kosher) salt and freshly ground pepper to taste)

◆ Steam vegetables in a vegetable steamer until just tender, about 10 minutes. (2 batches if necessary).

◆ Arrange in a shallow layer in a large baking dish or pan. Sprinkle with coarse salt and pepper.

◆ One hour before roast is due to come out of the oven, drizzle vegetables with beef drippings and toss to coat. Place in oven alongside the roast. Stir every 15 minutes or so.

◆ Leave vegetables in oven for the time the roast is standing. (Total cooking time, about 1 hour 15 minutes).

Grub Club Tip

A turkey baster is perfect for drawing the pan juices from the roasting pan.

YORKSHIRE PUDDING

The traditional English accompaniment to roast beef, this version is baked in a muffin tin for neat, individual servings.

⅓ cup beef drippings from roast	Pinch salt
1 clove garlic, minced	2 large eggs, room temperature
1 shallot, minced	⅔ cup water
1 cup flour	⅔ cup milk

◆ With a pastry brush, lightly coat muffin cups with beef drippings. Set aside.

◆ Heat 3 tablespoons of the drippings in a small skillet over medium-high heat. Add garlic and shallot. Sauté for 2 to 3 minutes until softened.

◆ Combine flour, salt, eggs, the water, milk, and remaining beef drippings in a medium bowl. Mix with an electric mixer on low speed until thoroughly blended. Stir in cooked garlic and shallot.

◆ Fill muffin cups ⅔ full with batter. Place muffin tin in oven one half hour before roast is done and bake until golden-brown and puffed.

Wine
The rich flavors of the dishes in this course demand a full-bodied, fruity red wine, such as a Washington Merlot. A Cabernet-Merlot would be another excellent choice.

◆ ACT IV ◆

SHERRIED FRUIT TRIFLE

A trifle is a sumptuous layered concoction, consisting of cake, spirits, fruit, custard, and whipped cream. It is traditionally served in a "trifle bowl"—a footed glass bowl with straight sides that show off the lovely layers. Any large glass bowl with relatively straight sides will work, or you may assemble the layers in individual stemmed wine glasses, ready for serving.

1 7-ounce pound cake, sliced ½-inch thick

½ cup cream sherry

2 10-ounce packages frozen raspberries, thawed and drained

1 15-ounce can sliced peaches, drained

1 cup whipping cream

2 Tbsp. sugar

1 tsp. vanilla

Custard

¼ cup sugar

3 Tbsp. flour

2 cups milk

3 egg yolks, beaten

2 tsp. finely grated lemon peel

1 tsp. vanilla

Candied Almonds

1 Tbsp. butter

½ cup sliced almonds

2 Tbsp. sugar

◆ For the candied almonds, melt the butter in a small skillet over medium-high heat. Stir in almonds and 1 tablespoon sugar. Cook, stirring constantly until sugar is dissolved and almonds are golden-brown. Sprinkle with remaining sugar and spread on a piece of waxed paper to cool.

◆ To make the custard, combine the ¼ cup sugar and the flour in a medium saucepan. Stir in the milk, egg yolks, and lemon peel. Cook over medium heat, stirring constantly, until the mixture coats a spoon (7 to 8 minutes). Remove from heat and stir in the 1 teaspoon vanilla. Transfer to a bowl to cool; place a sheet of plastic wrap directly onto the surface of the custard to prevent a skin from forming.

◆ To assemble the Trifle, cut or tear the slices of pound cake into 1-inch pieces. Place half in the bottom of the bowl or glasses and drizzle with one half of the sherry. Layer with one half of the custard, then the raspberries. Arrange the rest of the pound cake on top of the raspberries and sprinkle with the remaining sherry. Layer with the rest of the custard and top with the sliced peaches. Cover and refrigerate at least 4 hours.

◆ Before serving, whip the cream with the 2 tablespoons sugar and the 1 teaspoon vanilla. Spread over the top of the Trifle. Garnish with the candied almonds.

Grub Club Tip

Trifles offer lots of opportunity for creativity. Try different fruits, such as strawberries or blackberries, and spirits, such as rum or flavored brandies. Garnishes may include whole fresh berries, candied cherries, or chocolate curls.

Coffee

A cup of fresh-brewed coffee is certainly a wonderful accompaniment to the Trifle. However, for a change of pace, offer your guests a proper cup of hot tea (Earl Grey, perhaps) served with their choice of cream or wedges of lemon.

Curtain Call

The cream sherry you used in your Trifle also serves as a dessert wine. (The word "cream" in sherry terminology means "sweet"). It is served in small quantities, at room temperature or over ice. Its smooth, nutty flavor is perfect with fruit desserts, though some guests may prefer something fruitier, such as ruby port.

NOTES

MAIL-ORDER RESOURCE GUIDE

Blake's Natural
505 N. Railroad Avenue
Ellensburg, WA 98926
1-800-932-HERB • FAX: 1-509-925-4372

Healthy, tasty, "non-irradiated" herbs and spices, plus cookbooks and kitchen gear.

Cook Book
P.O. Box 88
Steuben, ME 04680

Bi-monthly newsletter for "cooks who read." Cookbook reviews, features, and recipes. Well-written and informative. Write for subscription information.

McCarthy And Schiering Wine Merchants
2209 Queen Anne Avenue North
Seattle, WA 98109
(206) 282-8500 • FAX (206) 524-0310

Daniel McCarthy, noted wine expert, is the author of "Pick the Right Wine"—the first-ever wine buying guide arranged by food to answer all of your "Which wine do I serve with—" questions. Indispensable! $10.00, plus $2.00 shipping and handling.

Morant Olive Oil
25 Ansonia Street
Hartford, CT 06114
1-203-724-4498

Highest quality 100% Spanish extra-virgin olive oil, imported since 1936. Taste the difference!

Spices, Etc.

P.O. Box 5448
Charlottesville, VA 22905
1-800-827-6373 • FAX: 1-800-827-0145

Spices, spice blends, flavorings, and sauces for all types of cooking, plus fabulous gift assortments.

Starbuck's Coffee Company

2203 Airport Way South
Seattle, WA 98134
1-800-455-3428 • FAX: (206) 622-2018

The world's best coffee delivered right to your door. Order their delightful catalog for a complete coffee education.

Sunburst Bottle Company

7001 Sunburst Way
Citrus Heights, CA 95621
Phone/fax: (916) 722-4632

Bottles, jars, and containers in all shapes and sizes for your "gifts from the kitchen" and home canning projects.

Teahouse Choice

1707 N. 45th Street Suite 101
Seattle, WA 98103
1-800-582-6946

Direct importers of the world's finest quality teas. Thirty-five different teas and tea blends to choose from.

R

Raita 143
Ratatouille 97
Raspberry Butter 48
Raspberry Sauce 17
Rice
  Basmati with Peas 142
  with Cuban Black Beans 88
  Steamed 63
Ruby Relish 24
Rumaki 23

S

Salads
  Christmas 156
  Garden Sunshine 51
  Greek 111
  Green Bean and Mushroom 99
  Island Shrimp 86
  Molded Waldorf 73
  Scrimmage 13
  Tossed Elegante 25
Salsa, Festive Fruit 89
Samosas 137
Satay, Pork 60
Scones, Orange Currant 47
Scrimmage Salad 13
Sesame Chicken Stir-Fry 62
Shamrock Dip 35
Sherried Fruit Trifle 161
Shrimp, Island Salad 86
Soups
  Chilled Strawberry Melon 49
  Colcannon 37
  Crab and Corn Chowder 125
  Mulligatawny 139
Souvlakia 113
Sparkling Pink Punch 72

Spiced Cucumber Wedges 138
Spicy Peanut Sauce 61
Spiked Gator Bowl 11

◆ Spring Fling 43
Spring Rolls 59
Squash, Creamed Butternut 128
Standing Rib Roast 158
Steamed Rice 63
Stew, Kelli's Irish 39
Strawberry Melon Soup, Chilled 49
Superbowl Sundaes 16
Super Brownies 16

◆ Superbowl Sunday 7
Super Duper Meat Loaf 75

T

◆ Taste of Thailand 55
Thai Dipping Sauce 60
Thai Iced Coffee 64
Touchdown Chicken Wings 12
Tossed Salad Elegante 25
Trifle, Sherried Fruit 161
Turkey, Maple Glazed Roast 126
Tzatziki 109

V, W

Vegetables, Oven Roasted 159
Wassail 155
Wild Rice Stuffing 127

Y, Z

Yorkshire Pudding 160
Zesty Hot Sauce 12

GOURMET GRUB CLUB PRODUCTS

Proudly display your Gourmet Grub Club spirit! Treat yourself, club members, family and friends with these fun and functional kitchen essentials.

Canvas Carry-All

This roomy, rugged carry-all is indispensable for trips to the grocery store, the library, or for toting gear to your Grub Club events. Environmentally friendly, 100% cotton canvas with sturdy webbed handles. Green Gourmet Grub Club logo. A terrific gift! $12.95.

Chef's Apron

The perfect kitchen cover-up! Professional quality chef's apron in easy-care 50% cotton, 50% polyester with adjustable neck strap and two handy pockets. Gourmet Grub Club logo in green. One size fits all. $14.95.

Hot Pads

No kitchen is complete without these handsome hot pads. Crisp white with red trim, quilted backs and loops for hanging. Black Gourmet Grub Club logo. Single: $4.95, pair: $7.95

ORDER FORM

Please send me:

_____ copies of *Creative Theme Parties*, $12.95 each $ _____

_____ copies of *The Gourmet Grub Club: A Guide to Cooking
          and Entertaining With Your Friends*, $12.95 each $ _____

_____ Canvas Carry-All, $12.95 each $ _____

_____ Chef's Apron, 14.95 each $ _____

_____ Hot Pads, single $4.95, pair $7.95 $ _____

                              Merchandise Total $ _____

Shipping and Handling($2.00 for orders up to $10.00.
Add $1.00 per each additional $10.00 of merchandise). $ _____

Washington state residents add 8.2% sales tax $ _____

                              TOTAL _____

❑ Check   ❑ Money Order

Ship To:

Name _____

Address _____

City _____ State _____ Zip _____

___ I do not wish to order anything at this time. However, please register
me in the International Gourmet Grub Club. (No purchase necessary).

Mail To:
TSI
111 James Street
Edmonds, WA 98020
Phone (206) 672-2963
Fax (206) 775-5727

NOTES

NOTES

Notes

_____

_____

_____

_____

_____

_____

_____

_____

_____

_____

_____

_____

_____

_____

_____

_____

_____

_____

_____

_____

_____

_____

_____

_____

_____

_____

NOTES

NOTES

NOTES

NOTES

NOTES

◆   ◆   ◆   ◆   ◆   ◆   ◆   ◆   ◆   ◆

On back cover...

The Gourmet Grub Club celebrating good food and good times. From left to right: Paula Prebezac, Kelli Ambrosi, Nick Prebezac, Chris Fabrizio, Shari Shields, Dan Ambrosi, and Jonathan Shields. Seated in front: Martine Fabrizio.